Civil Government

CIVIL GOVERNMENT:

AN

EXPOSITION OF ROMANS XIII. 1—7.

BY

JAMES M. WILLSON, A.M.

PHILADELPHIA:
WILLIAM S. YOUNG, 173 RACE STREET.
1853.

ADVERTISEMENT.

This volume contains the substance of Lectures delivered upon Romans xiii. 1–7, in the course of a regular exposition of this Epistle, and is published in pursuance of the following resolution adopted at a special meeting of the Cherry Street Reformed Presbyterian Congregation, Philadelphia.

"*Resolved*—That Mr. Willson be requested to furnish a copy of said Lectures for publication, and that Messrs. Wm. Cochran, David Smith, and John L. Keys, be a committee to attend to said publication."

CIVIL GOVERNMENT.

~~~~~~~~~~~~~~~~~~~~~~

Preface.

THE subject of civil government is, in all
its aspects, of no little importance. It occupies a large share of men's thoughts in all
enlightened countries, and awakens, just now,
the liveliest concern. This is not strange;
for its influence is felt in every department
of human action. It has to do with the peace,
the order, the material prosperity of the commonwealth; with the rights and liberties of
the citizens, and exercises no inconsiderable
influence upon the interests of morals and religion. In all these respects, in the last particularly, the institution of civil government
is deserving the attention of the Christian and
of the Christian minister. Moreover, the in-

1

spired writers take occasion, not unfrequent-
ly, to state, sometimes summarily in the doctrinal form, and sometimes in narrative and
in detail, leading principles by which the intelligent and faithful may be directed as to
the part which they are to take in setting up,
in administering, or in supporting political
constitutions. Hence, no apology is necessary in entering upon such an examination as
that which is now proposed. The topic itself
is of great moment, and the light and authority of God's Word are before us.

Again: these researches are imperatively
called for, inasmuch as the particular passage
to which the attention of the reader is asked
—Rom. xiii. 1—7—has been grievously per-
verted. One class of expositors endeavour to
derive from these teachings of Paul the offensive principle of unresisting, unquestioning subjection to civil authority of whatever
stamp. Rulers, say they, may be ungodly,
tyrannical, immoral,—they may use their
power for the worst ends,—they may subvert
the liberties, and take away the rights of
their subjects. Still, but one course is open;

even to such rulers and to such authority, there must be yielded at least a "passive obedience;" no "resistance" is ever lawful, though made by the entire body of the oppressed, and that under peril of eternal damnation: for "the powers that be are ordained of God; and he that resisteth the power receiveth unto himself damnation."

This principle was a very prominent topic among the controversies that arose in England after the restoration of Charles II., in 1660. The advocates of high Episcopacy—particularly the Oxford theologians—stated it in the strongest terms, maintaining the divine right of the restored government to an unlimited allegiance. It was revived, after the Revolution of 1688, by the non-jurors and their friends, who urged it against that settlement of affairs. The conflict raged long and was very bitter; for all, whether in church or state, who favoured the expulsion of James II., and the establishment of the succession to the throne in the house of Brunswick,—the friends of civil liberty,—were equally earnest in maintaining the right of a nation to take measures for the prevention of tyranny and of an arbitrary power over the rights of the subjects. All these, including such men as Burnet and Hoadly—while they vindicated monarchy as the best form of government, in this agreeing with their opponents, were no less vehement in asserting and also in proving that the apostle's doctrine implied certain limitations; that it must be interpreted so as not to conflict with the plain dictates of reason, or the liberties of nations. This form of the controversy regarding this celebrated passage, has passed away. Even Oxford found it impossible to carry out its own doctrine; and hence when James II. attempted to lay violent hands upon its chartered rights and immunities, Oxford resisted: it eat its own words, and took rank with the most decided adversaries of that Popish king in his assaults upon English law and Protestantism. While power was in the hands of a court professedly Protestant, and zealous for the ecclesiastical supremacy of the Church of England, it was all well enough; but when a new government arose which sought to transfer all the posts of honour and influence in church and state into popish hands, these conscientious defenders of an absolute divine right took the alarm, and refused to be bound by their own repeatedly asserted doctrines. After the Revolution, this principle did not outlast that generation which felt itself chagrined at the toleration of dissenters from the established religion. They had fought at a disadvantage, and lost ground. A new generation arose, and at last, as a topic of controversy, the subject was dropped, and hence, whatever private views may have been since entertained by the more bigoted loyalists and ecclesiastics, it has long ceased to figure in the annals of literature.

However, even the "exploded" doctrine of "non-resistance" has not entirely succumbed. It has found a place in the commentaries of Haldane and Chalmers, and still lingers in some minds; at least, in the form of doubts as to the propriety and lawfulness of setting aside institutions and men—by violence, if necessary,—that have proved themselves incompetent to answer the ends of political arrangements and authority.

There is another class of expositors, embracing a large proportion of the more modern, and some of the ancient, commentators; who, while they admit that nations may remodel their constitutions so as to suit themselves, and even resort to violence for the overthrow of tyrannical power—in other words, they admit the right of revolution—still hold and teach, as the doctrine of this passage, that so long as a government exists, whatever be its character, it is entitled to, and may demand, in the name of God, a conscientious obedience to its laws, unless they conflict with the laws of God.

This is a view highly plausible and popular, and yet to say nothing, at present, of its inconsistency, (for, how could there be a revolutionary movement, unless conscience had previously ceased to feel any obligation to respect and honour and fear the existing government?) it will appear in the sequel that it gains no countenance from the teachings of Paul, and for the reason that the passage makes no reference, as we think will appear upon strict examination of its terms, to any "power" but that which answers in some good measure the ends of its institution. Whatever may be the regard, if any, due to an immoral and tyrannical, and, of course, hurtful government, this passage makes no reference to it. It teaches one set of truths, and one only,—the nature, functions, and claims of a good government. In the language of Bishop Hoadly: "As the apostle's words stand at present, and have ever stood, it is impossible to prove that he had in view any particular magistrate acting against the ends of his institution;" and again, "All that we can possibly collect from his (Paul's,) injunctions in this place is this, that it is the indispensable duty of subjects to submit themselves to such governors as answer the good ends of their institution. There is nothing to make it probable that Paul had any governors particularly in his eye, who were a terror to good works and not to evil; or that he had any other design in this place but to press submission to magistrates, upon those who acknowledged none to be due in point of conscience, from the end of their institution, and the usefulness of their office. And in whatever instances submission can be proved to be due from this argument, I am ready to acknowledge that Paul extended it to all such instances. But as for submission in other instances, the apostle's reasoning here cannot defend or justify it, but rather implies the contrary. For if submission be a duty because magistrates are carrying forward a good work, the peace and happiness of human society, which is the argument Paul useth, it is implied in this that resistance is rather a duty than submission, when they manifestly destroy the public peace and happiness."

We are aware that the truth of these assertions remains to be proved: their truth will appear in the analysis of the passage, but we would now state it distinctly and emphatically, for it is the key to the right understanding of this, and parallel passages. Keeping this in mind, the scope and bearing of Paul's doctrine on civil government and

* Hoadly's Submission to the Powers that be; pages 49, 22, 50.

submission to authority, is as clear as a sunbeam. He gives no countenance to any slavish doctrine—to any claim of divine right to do wrong—to any principle that would tie up our hands, or in the least interfere with the right of the Christian citizen to "prove," by moral and scripture rules, as well as by the laws of self-preservation, any and all institutions and laws. In what light we are to regard tyrannical and ungodly powers, we may ascertain elsewhere, but cannot here, except, and the exception is important, that inasmuch as Paul gives us the character of government, *as God approves it*, and then enjoins subjection, we can pretty directly infer that in case a government does not possess, at least, a due measure of the requisite qualifications, the command to obey cannot apply to it.

A greater interest is, moreover, to be attached to such investigations as we propose, from the fact that the infidels of our times make use of this passage to serve their own purposes. We live in an age and country of liberal ideas regarding government—an age when the rights of the people are watched with the utmost sagacity and vigilance.— Popular rights are matters taken for granted, and any thing that runs counter to them is at once rejected. Infidelity attempts to turn this feeling in behalf of liberty into its own channel—to rouse it against the Bible, as if it favoured absolute and irresponsible power; and they avail themselves, and with no little success, of the mistaken exposition of the very passage before us. The expositors to whom we have referred intend to strengthen the arm of any and all civil authority—these interpretations the infidel school use for the overthrow of the authority of the Bible. Both are met and foiled by one process—simply by a just analysis of the passage itself.

This we now proceed to attempt, hoping to demonstrate, on the one hand, that a good government finds here both a guide and a pillar—and on the other, that a bad government finds not the faintest shadow of countenance, but is inferentially, but not the less effectually, condemned.

EXPOSITION OF ROMANS XIII. 1—7.

~~~~~~~~~~~~~~~~~~~~~~~~~~~~~~

"LET every soul be subject unto the higher powers.—
For there is no power but of God: the powers that be are
ordained of God. Whosoever therefore resisteth the power,
resisteth the ordinance of God; and they that resist shall
receive to themselves damnation. For rulers are not a
terror to good works, but to the evil. Wilt thou then
not be afraid of the power? Do that which is good,
and thou shalt have praise of the same. For he is the
minister of God to thee for good. But if thou do that
which is evil, be afraid, for he beareth not the sword
in vain: for he is the minister of God; a revenger, to execute wrath upon him that doeth evil. Wherefore ye
must needs be subject, not only for wrath, but also for
conscience sake. For for this cause pay ye tribute also;
for they are God's ministers, attending continually upon
this very thing. Render, therefore, to all their dues:
tribute to whom tribute is due—custom to whom custom
—fear to whom fear—honour to whom honour."

THIS passage will be found, upon careful analysis,
to embrace the following topics:

I. The duty in general of obedience to civil authority: v. 1.

II. General considerations enforcing this obedience: v. 1 and 2.

III. The design of the appointment of rulers, or of the institution of government: v. 3.

IV. The application of these principles to the case both of good and bad citizens: v. 3, 4.

V. The principle of obedience to civil rule: v.5,

VI. A more specific statement of the duties owing to civil government, as previously described; v. 6, 7.

SECTION I.

THE DUTY, IN GENERAL, OF OBEDIENCE TO CIVIL AUTHORITY.

"LET every soul be subject to the higher powers." verse 1.

1. *Civil governments are called "Powers."* The term here used (ε ξ ο υ σ ι α) is employed to denote any species of authority—paternal, ecclesiastical, magisterial. That in this instance it means civil rule, is abundantly clear from the whole tenor of the passage. It is important, however, to remark that it designates civil government, not as an institution endued with ability to execute its will—for this another term (δ υ ν α μ ι ς) would have been more appropriate—but as invested with the right to enact and administer law. "By what authority," (ε ξ ο υ σ ι α) say the scribes to our Lord, "doest thou these

things?"—"who hath given thee this authority?" (Matt. xxi. 23.*)

2. *They are called "Higher Powers."* The word (υπερεχουσαις) here rendered "higher," properly signifies prominence, or eminence, and hence it comes to mean "excellent," or "excelling," and must be translated by these or equivalent expressions in a number of passages in the New Testament. "Let each esteem other better (υπερεχοντας) than themselves," (Phil. ii. 3.) "And the peace of God, which passeth (υπερεχουσα) all understanding," (Phil. iv. 7.) "For the excellency (δια το υπερεχον) of the knowledge of Christ Jesus my Lord," (Phil. iii. 8.) In fact, the passage now before, us, and Pet. ii. 13, a parallel passage, are the only instances in which our translators have furnished a different rendering. Hence, some expositors have been disposed to lay no little stress upon this epithet, as distinctly defining the character of the'powers here intended, and as limiting to such the subjection here enjoined, the "excelling powers;" that is, powers possessing a due measure of the qualifications requisite to the rightful exercise of the power of civil rule.

That such is the fact—that the duty of subjection to civil rule is not absolutely unlimited—that

* See Appendix A.

it must be determined by other and higher considerations than the *mere* fact that it exists and
brandishes "the sword," is a most important truth
—a truth no where taught more clearly, as we shall
find, than in the passage before us. Still we are
not disposed to insist upon any different rendering.
We neither deny nor affirm. To elicit the true
meaning and import of the passage does not require
the aid of minute, and, after all, doubtful criticism.*
Civil rule is a "higher" power—it is invested with
an eminent dignity. It spreads its ægis—when
properly constituted and administered—over the
whole commonwealth, with all its varied interests,
and claims an unopposed supremacy. There is an
inherent majesty in lawful governmental power calculated and designed to impress subjects and citizens of every class and character with a salutary
awe. And whether the attributes of inherent
moral excellency be expressed in the designation
here given or not, it may be readily inferred, for
"power," without moral character, is a monster indeed.

It is, however, government and not the particular magistrates by whom authority is exercised, to
which Paul here refers. The distinction is important. "Rulers" are mentioned for the first time in

* See Appendix B.

v. 3. He now treats of the *institution* of civil rule. The "powers"—the "higher" powers,—Government in the abstract—the institution of civil rule.

3. *Subjection is enjoined to civil government;* v. 1: "Be subject:" that is, voluntarily, freely, and cheerfully rendering allegiance and homage, and yielding a uniform and conscientious obedience to the wholesome laws enacted by the "higher powers." In other words, what is here meant is something far different from an unresisting submission to what cannot be helped, as when the unarmed traveller submits to be despoiled by the highway robber. This kind of submission is, indeed, often called for. The slave must, of necessity, do the bidding of his master. The power is unjust. It may be tyrannically exercised. It is, in its very nature, despotic. But the victim of wrong has, for the time, no alternative. By obedience alone can he secure exemption from greater suffering. So the unhappy subject of arbitrary civil rule. He is beneath the iron heel of the despot. He must obey. But it is a forced obedience, wrung from him by the irresistible might of the tyrant's sceptre. So, also, the Christian may be compelled to yield a kind of submission to overwhelming power. He is in its hand. The sword is ready to enforce the mandates of unholy authority. The slave, and the sub-

ject of despotic civil rule, alike submit; but both
for the same reason—the impossibility of escape, or
of successful resistance.

To nothing of all this does the inspired apostle
here refer.   He employs a term ($\upsilon\pi o\tau\alpha\sigma\sigma\epsilon\sigma\theta\omega$)
that denotes an orderly and due submission—a
genuine and hearty subjection; and to fix the meaning of the injunction beyond dispute, he defines it
more fully, afterwards, in verses 5 and 7: "Wherefore ye must needs be subject, not only for wrath,
but also for conscience' sake: fear to whom fear—
honour to whom honour."   In short, whatever may
be the duty of the oppressed, and whatever his
rights, Paul does not here consider either.   He
deals with but one topic: the duty of subjection to
civil government—civil government as he afterwards describes it, with its duties, its character and
its claims.   To such a government there is due, not
mere obedience, but an obedience hearty and
prompt; an obedience importing an acknowledgment of its being and authority—an obedience originating in an intelligent perception and apprecia-
tion of its character, design, and happy fruits.   But
even this, we may safely say, is not inconsiderate
or unlimited, for it is an obedience limited, after all,
by the paramount claims of the law of God.   For
surely none but an atheist can deliberately affirm

that even the law of the land can set aside, weaken or nullify the authority of the law of God. To the *best* government, obedience can be yielded only in things lawful; for there is a "higher law" to which rulers and subjects are alike amenable. "The heavens do rule." There is a God above us, and "to Him every knee shall bow, and every tongue shall confess that Jesus Christ is Lord, to the glory of God the Father," (Phil. ii. 10, 11.) And, surely, if obedience to the best government is thus limited, it need hardly be added, that submission to an unholy power does not go beyond this. This also is limited by the law of God. It can only be yielded when this can be done without sin. In every other case, the subject—the slave even—should imitate the noble example of Daniel, and of myriads of the faithful before and since, and suffer rather than sin.

To return: the duty here inculcated is that of a hearty recognition of a rightful civil authority, together with an active support of its claims, and a personal and respectful obedience to its lawful enactments.

4. *This injunction lies upon every citizen.* "Let every soul be subject," &c.* (v. 1.) There is no

* We might, perhaps, have adduced this clause—the

exception. The rich and the poor, the young and the old, the Christian and the infidel, the minister of Christ as well as the private member of the church must be subject. In this lies much of the emphasis of the apostle's language; for it is clearly intended to rebuke the notion, early entertained, and that has still found a place among the professed followers of Christ, that it is unworthy of a Christian to be subject to civil rule; that having one master, even Christ, obedience is due, in no sense, not even with suitable limitations, to any other authority; and, also, to confute, before-hand, the arrogance of the popish priesthood, who claim, as all know, exemption from civil control. Equally opposed to both these is the explicit declaration of Paul, "Let *every soul* be subject to the higher powers."

Nor can this be wrested to the establishment of any authority on the part of the civil magistrate over the church of Christ. The church is an independent society. Her constitution, her doctrines, her laws, her administration, all are from Christ. To him alone is she subject. She exists, indeed, among and in the kingdoms of the world, but owns

term "soul" particularly—as an argument confirming our interpretation of the command, "be subject." It is not outward submission merely, but a subjection in which the "soul" goes along with the external act.

no allegiance to any other Head than to Christ. To claim supremacy over her is a presumptuous and unwarranted usurpation; God alone is Lord of the conscience.

INFERENCES.

1. Christians should endeavour to understand, and should take suitable interest in the subject of civil government. It is neither remote from them, nor too unholy to occupy their attention. From the mere contests of faction they may, indeed, stand aloof; but, surely, that which attracted the attention of an inspired apostle is not beneath the study of the most spiritually-minded of the followers of Christ. He should study the subject, moreover; for without this, he cannot with becoming high intelligence perform his own duty respecting it.

2. The Christian minister may and ought to present the doctrine of the word of God, on this, as on other subjects of which the inspired writers treat. The time was, when it would have been necessary to argue elaborately in defence of this statement. It is not necessary now. The pulpit has been compelled to enter this field—long almost abandoned. An age of, at least, attempted social reformation, has driven every party in turn to seek the powerful aid of the Christian ministry, and while we cannot

in many instances find much to commend in the manner in which the subject has been presented, it is still so far well, that portions of the Word of God which exhibit the character, functions, and claims of civil power, are no longer regarded as forbidden ground. Still, there is need of wisdom. In such discussions, the ambassador of Christ should keep close to the footsteps of his Master and of his inspired followers, and rising above the transient conflicts and unworthy behests of party, should essay to exhibit and illustrate the entire subject of governmental arrangements and polity, in a manner becoming an exalted moral institution—so as to bring a revenue of glory to Christ the Supreme Lawgiver.

SECTION II.

GENERAL CONSIDERATIONS ENFORCING THE DUTY OF OBE- DIENCE TO CIVIL RULE.

"For there is no power but of God: the powers that be are ordained of God. Whosoever, therefore, resisteth the power, resisteth the ordinance of God; and they that resist shall receive to themselves damnation." Verses 1, 2.

HAVING stated the duty, the apostle now proceeds to show the grounds on which it rests, insisting upon two classes of arguments, and

1. *They derive their power from God*, or in other words, government is a divine institution, originating in, and, of course, sanctioned by the will of God. For (1.) "There is no power but of God." This is true, whatever sense we attach to the word "power." All physical power—all executive energy, in every department of creation, is from God. "In Him we live, and move, and have our being." (Acts xvii. 28.) In this sense the power of evil beasts and even of the devil, is from God. "By Him all things consist," (Col. i. 17.) Again, if we understand by "power," the possession of the reins of government, it is, certainly, through Him that kings are permitted to occupy their thrones and that, whatever the steps by which they may have succeeded to the seat of authority. Pharaoh was "raised up" in the course of that providence which controls all the affairs of men. God "gave the kingdom" to Jeroboam. The same hand "raised up" Cyrus, and our Lord expressly declares to Pilate, the unholy Roman governor, "Thou couldest have no power at all against me, except it were given to thee from above," (John xix. 11.) Even the devil has "power," in this sense, from God. Does Paul mean no more than this? Assuredly he means something far different. This clause assigns a reason for that hearty subjec-

tion which the apostle had just enjoined. But, surely, the mere fact that one possesses "power," can be no reason why his claims should be acknowledged, and his laws conscientiously obeyed. If so, the slave—ay, the slave who has been stolen from his own land and ignominiously held as a chattel—would be required to admit, as from God, the validity of his master's claims. To throw off his chains, and make his way to his native home as a freeman, would be rebellion against God. No doctrine could be more agreeable than this to tyrants, and to all the panders to unholy power; for, if this be Paul's meaning, there is no despot, no usurper, no bloody conqueror, but could plead the divine sanction, and, more than this, the devil himself could lay the teachings of Paul under contribution to enforce his pre-eminently unholy authority. An interpretation which leads to such monstrous conclusions—that would bind the nations to the footstool of power with iron chains, and utterly crush every free aspiration—that would invest with the sanctions of the divine name the most flagrant usurpation and the most unrelenting despotism—stands self-condemned.

But we go further. Providence is not a rule of action. Sin and evil of all kinds exist in the course of the same providential administration, as that which furnishes a place for governments which contemn God and oppress mankind. And yet who claims for sin a divine *sanction?* who denies to the suffering the right to rid themselves of their trials? Carry out this interpretation, and you furnish the bloody government of the Papal states an impregnable defence against the efforts of the liberators of Italy.

The truth is, the apostle has no reference here at all to any thing but the *institution* of government;* and designs to assert, and does assert, that there is no authority properly exercised over men, but that which God has established. This is true in the largest sense: for man is God's creature and subject, and he who sets up claims to dominion over him must be prepared to show that he exercises an authority of that sort and of that character which bears the stamp and sanction of divine institution. Had Paul, indeed, said no more, it might have been argued, with greater plausibility, that he designed in this passage to give the tyrants of the earth, what they have always claimed, the sanction of the

* "*Power* is to be distinguished from *persons;* for Paul loved polity and power; but Caligula and Nero he execrated as monsters in nature, instruments of the devil, and pests of the human race." Lectures on Romans by Andrew Melville, Edin., 1850, p. 487.

Most High in their course of monstrous iniquity. Even then, however, we would have endeavoured, and we think successfully, to vindicate the word of God against so abhorrent a conclusion. But Paul did not stop with these general assertions. He proceeds, as will presently appear, to define, with great distinctness and brevity, his own meaning: to designate the sort of "power" to which he alludes: not any and *every* existing government, but that which answers the end of its institution. In short, the design of this clause: "There is no power but of God," is merely to assert the general principle that subjection is due to civil government, inasmuch as government is a divine institution. This appears more distinctly from what follows.

(2.) "The powers that be are ordained of God." The prime fallacy of many commentaries on this entire passage consists in taking for granted that this phrase—this celebrated phrase—"the powers that be"—means all and any existing governments. This cannot be. The considerations already advanced, in setting aside a similar interpretation of the preceding clause, forbid it. Nor are there wanting others, equally conclusive. Of Israel it is said, referring to the establishment of an independent government by the ten tribes under Jeroboam, "They have set up kings, but not by me; they

have made princes, and I knew (approved) it not."
(Hos. viii. 4.) And the prophet Daniel, and afterwards the apostle John, expressly and frequently
denominate the Roman Empire a "beast." The
former, a "beast, dreadful and terrible, and strong
exceedingly; and it had great iron teeth: it devoured and brake in pieces, and stamped the residue with the feet of it," (Dan. vii. 11.) The latter, a "beast having seven heads and ten horns,
and on its horns ten crowns, and on its heads the
name of blasphemy," (Rev. xvii. 1.) Surely
such a description was never given of a government
that could lay any solid claim to be "ordained of
God;" at least, in any other sense than the pes-
tilence is God's ordinance, existing in his providence, but to be shunned and banished as soon as
possible.* And, in fact, for this end, among

* "So are fevers, plagues, fires, inundations, tempests,
and the like. And yet Almighty God not only permits,
but requires us to use all prudent methods of resisting
and stopping their fury, but is far from expecting that we
should lie down, and do nothing to save ourselves from
perishing in such calamities. So likewise are robbers
and cut-throats God's judgments, but this doth not prove
that you must submit yourselves and families to be ruined
at their pleasure. So again are inferior magistrates, if
they make use of their power to fall with violence upon
their neighbours, and attempt their lives, or the ruin of

3

others, the gospel is sent into the world. It is the "stone cut out of the mountain without hands," which is to "smite the great image (Dan. ii.) and break it in pieces." One ordinance of God, smiting, and breaking in pieces, another! The term "powers" here denote, as before, the institution of civil rule. This, with all other kinds of power that may be lawfully exercised among men, is "ordained of God." In other words, the Most High has made provision for the exercise of civil authority. He has not left mankind to be controlled by no other government than that of parents over their children,

their families; and yet they may be resisted, and their illegal violence repelled by violence. And so, lastly, are foreign enemies and invaders, always reckoned amongst God's judgments, and amongst the most remarkable of them; and yet there is no necessity, I hope, from hence, of tamely submitting ourselves to them: and no argument from hence, against the lawfulness or honourableness of resisting them. Either, therefore, let it be shown, that this objection holds good in other of God's judgments; or, that there is something peculiar in this to exempt it from the common rule; or let it be acknowledged that it signifies nothing in the present case." *Hoadly's Submission to the Powers that be.* London, 1718, p. 85. Hoadly presents this, it will be seen, as an answer to the objection, that bad governments are to be submitted to, and not thrown off, because they are judgments of God. It comes in as well here.

of masters over their servants, of church rulers over private Christians. He has, also, provided for the setting up and administering of another kind of power, having its own peculiar ends, its rules, its limits, and its administrators—the power of civil government. God has willed the existence of a national organization and polity; and, in so doing, has fixed its ends, which it must subserve; has given it a supreme law, which it must observe; has bound it by limits which it may not pass over. In short, God has "ordained"* civil government as Christ has ordained the ministry of reconciliation, not by merely willing its existence, but by prescribing its duties, its functions, its ends, and its limitations.

No other meaning can be affixed to the language of the apostle, consistently with due reverence for Him who is the Holy One and the Just, the rightful and beneficent moral Governor. Can it be, for a moment, believed, that God has made man a social being—placed him in society, and thus necessitated, by the very laws of the human constitution, the establishment of civil rule, and that he has, after all, set no bounds to the authority, no

---

* The marginal translation, "ordered," is rather better than that of the text.

hedge about the claims of civil rulers? That, after all, He has left this whole matter to be *lawfully* managed, not by law, even His law, not by rule, but merely according to human caprice, or, what is far worse, human ambition, self-seeking, pride, and violence? And, then, as the issue of the matter, that in case a government exist, whatever the ends it aims at, whatever the principles that guide its administration, whether it be just or unjust, God-fearing or infidel, liberal or despotic, it exists, and He acknowledges it as "ordained" by Him, and as entitled to the regard, homage and obedience of its subjects? This cannot be. God is not so indifferent to His own glory, or to the welfare of man, and particularly of the church. He never intended, we may assert, with entire confidence, to sign, if we may so speak, a blank, and then leave man to fill it up according to his pleasure. Every attribute of God forbids this. Paul teaches no such doctrine.

The terms employed by the apostle, and the connexion of the clauses, accord precisely with these views. He first asserts "power is not, except from God:"* God alone is the source of legitimate authority. He is sovereign. Man is His. Power, not derived from God, is ever illegitimate. It is

---

* Ου γαρ εστιν εξουσια ειμη απο Θεου.

mere usurpation; as, for example, the Pope's claim to reign in the church, and over the nations. The apostle then adds, in vindication of civil government, "the powers that be"—governmental institutions; "are arranged under God,"* or if this be preferred, "by God." There is such a "power" as that of civil rule. It is among the kinds of authority for which the Most High has made provision, and to which he has assigned the requisite laws and functions.

But we rest our interpretation upon no mere verbal criticism. God is the only source of power. And God has in the sense in which we have explained the term, "ordained" civil government. He is the source of power, that power of which Paul speaks, not as He endows with physical

---

* Αι δε ουσαι εξουσιαι, υπο του Θεου τεταγμεναι εισιν. We here quote from the commentary of Andrew Melville. He says, "The third argument is taken from the order divinely constituted under God—for the glory of God; for so I interpret υπο του, &c. Not so much 'from God,' which has been already said, as 'powers are arranged under God.' Which with the article τας ουσας he calls εξουσιας —as if he had said τας οντως, &c., 'which are truly powers' and deserve the name. Whence, an impious and unjust tyranny, which is not of God, as such, nor accords with the divine order, he excludes, as illegitimate, from this legitimate obedience." Comment. p. 497.

3*

strength, or even as He opens the way, in his providence, for its successful employment in subjugating mankind; but as he has authorized the exercise of that particular kind of authority; of course,. putting upon it, when measurably conformed to his institution, the impress of His own dignity, and the sanction of His law.*

Is it inquired, where this institution is found? The reply has been, in part, anticipated. In the constitution of man, and in the principles of piety, of equity, of beneficence, originally implanted in the human heart, but now, much more clearly, in the written Scriptures, which abound with instruction, addressed to rulers and people, and furnishing all the light mankind need for the organization and administration of the most salutary political regimen. The passage before us is an example. It is proper, however, to add, that instruction is given in the word of God, not so much in regard to the particular form which the government should assume, as in reference to the ends it should seek, the principles that should guide the administration, and the character of those into whose hands national affairs should be committed.

* "And this may serve to explain yet farther in what sense these higher powers are from God; viz., as they

This is Paul's first argument enforcing the duty of obedience, and to demonstrate that it is not beneath the dignity of the Christian to be subject to civil government. So far from offending Christ, such subjection honours him—for it is yielded to a divine institution, and for the same reason, it cannot safely be withheld. Hence Paul argues

2. *From the sin and danger of resisting civil authority, and*

(1.) The sin. "Whosoever, therefore, resisteth the power, resisteth the ordinance of God."— Verse 2d.

The distinction is still kept up between the institution—"the ordinance" of God, and the magistrate in whose hands the reins of government happen to be found. "Whosoever resisteth the power." A most important distinction. For, in truth, there are occasions when it is not merely lawful, but a matter of high and imperative duty, to resist autho-

act agreeably to his will, which is, that they should promote the happiness and good of human society, which Paul all along supposes them to do. And consequently, when they do the contrary, they cannot be said to be from God, or to act by his authority, any more than an inferior magistrate may be said to act by a prince's authority, whilst he acts directly contrary to his will." Hoadly, p. 5.

rity. The case of the high priest, Azariah, and his brethren, who withstood Uzziah, king of Judah, in his attempt to pass over the limits of his power and obtrude into the priest's office, is well known to every reader of the Bible: "It pertaineth not unto thee, Uzziah, to burn incense unto the Lord; but to the priests, the sons of Aaron, that are consecrated to burn incense: go out of the sanctuary, for thou hast trespassed." (1 Chron. xxvi. 18.) And still more to the purpose are the cases of Shadrach, Meshech and Abednego, and afterwards of Daniel, who all refused compliance with laws enacted by the then supreme authority in Babylon (Dan. iii. vi.) To the same effect is the refusal of Peter and John to obey the command of the Jewish magistracy "not to speak at all, nor teach in the name of Jesus." They reply, "Whether it be right in the sight of God to hearken unto you more than unto God, judge ye," (Acts iv. 18, 19.) Indeed, until of late, the duty of refusing to obey the commands of the civil power, when they conflict with duty to God was never, so far as we know, denied by any bearing the name of Christian. It is certain that the advocates of the doctrine of "passive obedience and non-resistance" during the 17th and 18th centuries in England, did not go so far as this. The very terms in which they announced their doctrine make this manifest, "*passive* obedience, *non-resistance*." They acknowledged a higher law than the enactments of human, and, of course, fallible, and often impious power. The first prominent enunciation of the principle of unlimited and unquestioning obedience, was reserved for an atheist—Hobbes of Malmesbury. Denying the existence of any fixed standard of right—and, consequently, of any such things as virtue and vice—this speculative philosopher resolved all the laws of morality into one— the will of the legislature. But who were his disciples? None but the godless, the dissipated, the scorners of all that is sacred. The heart of England was shocked at the daring attempt to dethrone the Almighty. It was reserved for another age and another land to hear and assent to the blasphemous assertion, that the law of the land overrides all other laws, and *must* be obeyed under penalty of resisting the ordinance of God.

But we may go further, and assert that Paul did not intend, by the language before us, to forbid even the forcible resistance of unjust and tyrannical civil magistrates, not even when that resistance is made with the avowed design of displacing offending rulers, or, it may be, the change of the very form of the government itself. There are few in this land, or in any free country, to deny the right of a nation to rid itself of oppressive power —whether foreign or domestic. The right of revolution, for the purpose of throwing off usurping or tyrannical rule, need not, now and here, be defended. That question was settled in England by the Revolution of 1688, when the nation, rising in its might, expelled James II. as an enemy to the constitutional rights and liberties of the people. The separate national and independent existence of these United States is the fruit of successful revolution. And where is the American—the American Christian—who does not rejoice in the hope that the principles of liberty will spread and prevail, even though they be ultimately established upon the wreck of thrones demolished or overturned?

Does the Spirit of God here condemn these efforts of the nations to rid themselves of the yoke of despots? Does this passage rivet the chains of the oppressed? Certainly not. God denounces the oppressor. "Wo to him that buildeth his house by unrighteousness and his chambers by wrong," (Jer. xxii. 13.) "Wo unto them that decree unrighteous decrees, and that write grievousness, which they have prescribed." (Is. x. 1.) And, to say nothing of the threatenings—repeated and awful—against the ungodly and oppressing powers, symbolized by the "beast" of Daniel and of the Revelation, we have the striking inquiry of Psalm xciv. 20 : "Shall the throne of iniquity have fellowship with thee, which frameth iniquity by a law?"

Now is it credible that notwithstanding these denunciations, the Most High does still forbid, under penalty of his high displeasure, all conflicts for liberty? That he so far takes under his patronage ungodly governments which despise his law and his Son—as to regard any opposition to their authority as opposition made to his own holy "ordinance" of magistracy? To persuade us of this, we may first demand the clearest evidence.

It is evident that the proper interpretation of this passage depends upon the meaning of the phrase, "ordinance of God." What then is its import? Does it mean any and every existing government? Does it mean a Phocas, who "waded to the throne of the Roman Empire through seas of blood?" Does it mean that Joseph of Austria, with his government, is the "ordinance of God" to Hungary? Does it mean the government of the Pope and his cardinals, under which the Papal States groan? In short, is this term applied to any government merely from the fact that it exists?

Clearly not; for, then, the powers just mentioned must be also embraced in it—a conclusion equally repulsive to the Christian and to the friend of human liberty. And, besides, if this be its meaning, the *very worst* government has the very same right to demand an unresisting subjection, as the very best, for both alike exist—exist in the same over-ruling and all-controlling providence; and both would be armed with the same high sanction : to "resist" either, would be to make the same assault upon the "ordinance of God !"

What, then, is its import? The reply has been already anticipated.* It denotes God's *moral* ordinance of civil government—it refers to such a government as Paul afterwards describes—a government which is "a terror to evil-doers, and a praise to them that do well"—a government that in due measure answers the ends of the institution of civil rule, a government of law, of equity, possessed of moral attributes, and ruling "under God," by whom it has been "ordered," for the execution of high and useful functions.

Who, then, resists? The reply is at hand, and conclusive. He who opposes the rightful exercise of civil rule; he who would attempt the overthrow of just and wholesome authority; he who endea-

* See page 23.

vours to weaken the hands of the "higher powers" in their performance of the trust committed to them: he who rises against the restraints imposed upon the lawless, the profane: he who wilfully disturbs the peace, and interferes with the regular administration of justice: for such, and such alone, assail "the ordinance of God." Indeed, we may well ask how this can possibly apply to any but those who invade the good order of the commonwealth by opposing wholesome rule? The end for which governments were established is, surely, more important than government itself, and much more important than the particular form, or the mere fact of the possession of power by this individual or that. How, then, can any one be regarded as chargeable with the sin and crime of resisting God's "ordinance," who refuses to obey an unjust enactment, or who even goes so far as to attempt the overthrow of or remodelling of a government that is, by tyranny, or injustice, or ungodliness, working harm to society, and dishonour to God, and so tends to defeat the very ends for which the "ordinance" of civil rule was established? The commands of a maniac or drunken father may be disregarded—the wife or even the children taking the government into their own hands— much more may institutions and laws be disre-

4

garded when these run counter, either in their constitution or administration, to the divine law, and
thus tend to the manifest injury of the common
weal.*

But does not this tend to the enfeebling of the
claims of even legitimate authority? By no means.
True, all institutions administered by human hands
will, necessarily, bear the marks of human imper-
fection, and it may be difficult, in theory, to draw
the line, and say, this much is requisite to constitute a government on which we may inscribe the
title "the ordinance of God;" but, in practice, the
difficulty will not be often very great—no greater
than in many other departments of duty.   Surely,
we may go so far as to affirm, with confidence, that
every "ordinance of God" will acknowledge his
claims—the claims of His Son (we speak of governments in enlightened lands,) and the supremacy of His law, and will *seek* to promote the welfare of *all* the subjects or citizens.

* "Now this being the argument of the apostle, all that
we can possibly collect from his injunctions in this place
is this: That it is the indispensable duty of subjects to
submit themselves to such governors as answer the good
end of their institution; to such rulers as he here describes; such as are not a terror to good works, but to
the evil; such as promote the public good, and are continually attending upon this very thing." Hoadly, p. 7.

That this doctrine, moreover, is liable to be abused by the lawless, we admit. The opponents of the slavish principle of "passive obedience" encountered the same objection. Says Bishop Hoadly, "The great objection against this, though it be all founded upon the will of God, who sincerely desires the happiness of public societies, is this, that it may give occasion to subjects to disturb and oppose their superiors. But, certainly, a rule is not therefore bad, because men may mistake in the application of it to particular instances; or because evil men may, under the umbrage of it, satisfy their own passions and unreasonable humours; though these latter, as they are disposed to public disturbance, would certainly find out some other pretence for their behaviour, if they wanted this. The contrary doctrine to what I have been delivering, we know, by an almost fatal experience, may be very much abused; and yet that is not the reason why it ought to be rejected, but because it is not true. Every man is to give an account for his sins; and the guilt of those who, under any pretence whatsoever, disturb the government of such as act the part of good rulers, is so great, that there cannot be a stronger motive than this against resistance and opposition to such."* It may be

* Hoadly, pp. 10, 11.

added that every argument on behalf of civil liberty may also be abused, and equally, the doctrines of grace. And yet, after all, we need not much fear any liability to abuse in the application of this principle, provided it be rightly understood; for its very basis and groundwork is that God has ordained civil society and organization, and that existing institutions are only to be resisted when they fail to answer the ends for which government has been established among divine ordinances, while— and this is the apostle's argument—to "resist" a government which is really an "ordinance of God" is a sin of heinous character. This is plainly taught when Paul proceeds to enforce subjection,

(2.) *From the danger of resistance.* And they that resist shall receive to themselves damnation, (κριμα—condemnation,) v. 2. From what quarter? from the government, or from God? That the apostle designed no more than to assert the fact that such as impugn the authority of government, or resist its commands, or oppose themselves to its authority, will meet with civil punishment, does not appear probable. This would be to assert a fact too well known to require so emphatic and solemn an enunciation. Of course, no government will tamely allow its injunctions to be set at naught, so long as it bears the sword. And, moreover, it seems hardly consistent with the high and religious tone of the entire passage, to understand this clause as having no higher reference than to the infliction of civil punishment upon the disorderly and rebellious. What immediately precedes contains a pretty distinct intimation, as has already been remarked, of the fact that "resistance" to legitimate authority is not only a sin, but a sin of a heinous character. Nor are more express declarations to the same effect wanting elsewhere in the Word of God. We may refer to the case of Korah and the princes of Judah, whom God visited with a most signal token of his wrath for this very sin. "They went down alive into the pit." (Num. xvi.) And all remember the sad story of Absalom, who also died in the same sin in an attempt to overturn a lawful power.*

Still, we are not to infer that the sin of resisting civil rule involves necessarily eternal ruin. It deserves "condemnation." God sees it. It highly offends Him. He will vindicate his own "ordinance." And why not? If it be, as it certainly is, a most beneficial one—if it promote directly

---

* Hodge says, "Paul does not refer to the punishment which the civil magistrate may inflict, for he is speaking of disobedience to those in authority as a sin against God, which he will punish."

4*

every temporal interest, and, at least, indirectly bears upon the moral and religious welfare of the community—if successful resistance to good government opens the flood-gates to violence, irreligion, vice, and misery—if no interest can flourish when good laws are not well administered—can it be regarded as unworthy of the Divine Spirit to attach this emphatic sanction to the institution of civil rule—to assert, in this explicit form, that God will mark with his evident disapprobation every act of resistance to the righteóus exercise of magistratical power?

On these high grounds, then, does Paul enforce subjection to the "higher powers." Government is from God—to resist, is to resist his "ordinance," and "he that resists receives a righteous 'condemnation.' "*

INFERENCES.

1. *That civil government is, as an institution, from God.*—National organization is not the mere creature of the voluntary action of the inhabitants of a particular country or district. It is their province, indeed, to establish the particular institutions by which they are to be guided and governed; and in this sense, political arrangements are "the

* See Appendix C.

ordinance of man," (1 Pet. ii. 13.) Still, it is not optional with men whether such an institution as civil government exist at all. God has "ordained" it. And it is important to remark, that government once set up, its rights and prerogatives are not *wholly* determined by the popular will. To some extent they certainly are; but in others they, as certainly, are not. The Most High has fixed the leading ends of all civil rule;* and has also defined, to some extent, the means to be employed in effecting these. It is not optional, for example, with any people, whether they shall commit to the magistracy the power of inflicting death upon the murderer—the law of God determines this. It is a subtle question, and one that in some respects possesses a practical importance—whether civil power is, in the aggregate, a collection made up of contributions of rights thrown in by individual members of the commonwealth—each resigning a portion of his own. By no means. No man has a right to take his own life, and yet society has the right to inflict capital punishment, and, moreover, such a notion is entirely inadmissible on another ground. Man was made for society, and, hence,

---

* The fact, and what these ends are, will be the subject of our next section.

so far is he from being necessarily restricted in his rights in the social state, that it is as a member of society alone, that he can enjoy all the privileges and perform all the duties of manhood.

In short, while the people of a country have in their own hands the setting up of their government, and the choice of rulers—when this is once done, and *rightly done*—the authority by which the government is administered is to be regarded as derived from the divine institution of the ordinance of magistracy. Hence,

2. *The principal standard by which this institution is to be measured is the Word of God.*— This may be inferred directly from the fact that the scriptures treat so fully on the subject. It appears in each Testament, and in every form of instruction. There are didactic passages—such as that before us. Of this character are the teachings and the precepts of the moral law, which contains a complete exhibition of all that relates to the ends, the principles, the methods of civil rule—and much of the detail respecting magistratical duties, and their correlates, the duties of subjects and citizens. The narratives of the Bible largely illustrate its didactic rules and precepts. It abounds with exemplifications both of good and bad governments, and the issues of the one and of the other. Much

of prophecy, both of the Old Testament and of the New, is designed to shed light upon the subject of civil polity, and the divine administrations respecting it.

Where else can this be learned? Not from the light of nature merely. True, the essential principles of social organization, and even of political regimen, are contained in the moral law, and that law is the same that was inscribed upon the heart of man at his creation. But the "law of nature" is not to be confounded with the "light of nature" —the law as a complete rule of human duty is man's primitive condition—the light that is now in man is too feeble to discern it in any thing like its holiness and perfection. To reject the Word of God in this, as in any other department of duty, is, to use the words of John Brown of Haddington, "an obstinate drawing back to heathenism."

There is still another reason why we must refer to the Scriptures, and make them the supreme standard. There, and there alone, do we ascertain the *now* essential principle of right civil rule, the Headship of Jesus Christ: for "He is made head over all things to the church," (Eph. i. 22.) To Him "all judgment is committed," (John v. 22.) He is "Prince of the kings of the earth," (Rom. i. 5.) And not merely do we learn this fact, but having ascertained it, we are led at once to the conclusion that to His own Word must we now address ourselves, if we would become acquainted with that institution itself of which He so plainly claims the supremacy.

3. *Disorderly and seditious behaviour is here most signally rebuked.*—The ordinance of magistracy, rightly set up and administered, ranks among the most important: in some respects, it is first of the institutions with which men have to do. And social order is of itself "of great price." How wrong to disturb it by disorderly and lawless conduct. It is sometimes, indeed, a matter of no little moment to determine where the guilt lies! We would not style any either disorderly or seditious, who are contending in a right spirit against the corruptions of the State, or of the public administration of affairs. Sometimes the rulers themselves are the disturbers of the peace, and upon them falls the threatening of this passage. However, we now speak of the seditious and disorderly, of those who are such in a community where a scriptural magistracy and wholesome rule are in operation. These are to be regarded as chargeable with an offence of no inferior turpitude; as deserving of the most severe reprobation, and as fit subjects for punitive inflictions. And, it may be added, that the spirit of peace and

order should, as far as possible, characterize the
conduct of those who dissent from unholy and oppressive governments, and attempt their reformation.

SECTION III.

THE DESIGN OF THE APPOINTMENT OF CIVIL RULERS, OR OF THE INSTITUTION OF CIVIL GO-VERNMENT.

"For rulers are not a terror to good works, but to the
evil." Verse 3.

THIS and the subsequent section furnish us with
the key to the entire passage. Had the apostle
merely enjoined subjection to civil authorities, as
he does in the terms of verses first and second,
adding no explanations, giving no clue to the character of the power to which his injunction is designed to apply, it would have been difficult, perhaps impossible, *from the passage itself*, to have
shown any limitations—we might have been compelled to resort mainly to other Scriptures for light
as to the duty really, after all, enjoined. We
might, indeed, have obtained some light from the
term ($\varepsilon\xi o\upsilon\sigma\iota\alpha$,) and from the phrase ($\tau\varepsilon\tau\alpha\gamma\mu\varepsilon\nu o\iota$
$\upsilon\pi o$ $\tau o\upsilon$ $\Theta\varepsilon o\upsilon$:) we could have evaded the advocate

of "passive obedience and non-resistance," but we would almost have despaired of convincing him. But with the apostle's own explanations all is clear. He enjoins obedience, but he adds a reason drawn from the character of the power, and so limits, most clearly and conclusively, his own injunction: *"for rulers are not a terror to good works, but to the evil."*

1. *Paul here defines a government set up and engaged in attending to its appropriate functions:* "*Rulers* are not a terror," &c.   Hitherto, the subject has been *government*—civil government as a divine institution.   Here, for the first time, we meet with a direct reference to magistrates actually employed in administering the affairs of the commonwealth, including, of course, legislators, judges, and executive officers. This change of phraseology is not without design. It is clearly intended to establish a distinction—a distinction existing in the very nature of the case between the *institution* of government and governors themselves. The institution of government is to be studied, governors are to be tried, or, if the expression be more correct, the entire character and operations of government, as it actually exists, urges its claims upon the citizen and the Christian.

2. The governors to whom the injunction of

Paul applies *"are not a terror to good works."*
To what does Paul here refer? to what class of
"works?" Does this phrase mean no more, as
Tholuck explains it, than such works as are the
opposite of resistance and rebellion? Most certainly not. Such an interpretation puts an entirely
new meaning upon the phrase "good works," and
would, moreover, fix upon the apostle the charge
of expressing himself with an unaccountable ob-
scurity and meagreness. Does it mean such
"works" as industry, honesty, and the orderly
discharge of common, social, and relative duties?
No doubt these are included in it. But even this
is a very defective interpretation. There must be
added, at least, such things as come under the
head of common morality. But we go farther.
Paul here speaks, not as a mere heathen philosopher, but as a Christian minister, and an apostle
of Christ. What then are "good works?" The
answer is clear. They are such as the law of
Christ demands: they are all the external results
and fruits of the operations of the Spirit of Christ.
Among these, as already intimated, will be found
all that is comprehended under the name of morals;
but they include much more—Sabbath sanctifica-
tion, the public profession of the name and truth
of Christ—His worship, and efforts to advance his

5

kingdom and interest. Thus Eph. ii. 10. "Cre-
ated in Christ Jesus unto *good works.*" 2 Tim.
iii. 17. "That the man of God may be perfect,
thoroughly furnished unto all *good works.*" Tit.
ii. 14. "Zealous of *good works.*" 1 Tim. iii. 1.
"He that desireth the office of a bishop desireth a
good work." 2 Thess. ii. 17. "Stablish you in
every good word and *work;*" this good work being,
in part, what is referred to elsewhere in addressing
the Thessalonian church, that from them "the
word of the Lord had sounded out." Rev. ii. 26.
"And he that overcometh and keepeth *my* works
unto the end, to him will I give power over the
nations;" and, finally, Rev. xiv. 13. "Blessed are
the dead which die in the Lord—that they may
rest from their labours, and *their works* do follow
them."

It is not denied that, in most of these passages
and similar ones, works of morality are meant; but
in some, the immediate and only reference is to
"works" peculiarly denominated religious, and in
no instance can these be excluded. How can we
imagine that Paul departed, in the passage before
us, from the current meaning which every Christian attaches to this phrase.* Now, to such

* "For temporal princes—not to punish men for any
works that are good in themselves (like those which the

"works" magistrates—those referred to by the apostle—will not be "a terror." Against such as practise these, he will enact no laws. And does not the principle already taught, that magistracy is the "ordinance of God," abundantly confirm this? It is, in fact, a most serious error, and one that has led to many others, that God has ordained any institution among men, or sanctions any, in which the promotion of his glory as the Supreme Lawgiver, and the alone object of worship and religious homage, is not a *chief* end. "The Lord hath made all things for himself," Job xvi. 27. And of every people, in a certain sense, does God say, as He said with a peculiar emphasis of ancient Israel, and says of the church, "This people have I formed for myself, to show forth my praise." This is expressly asserted of the family relation, Mal. ii. 15. And as to government, who questions that among the patriarchs, all authority, including what we now term civil, was to be so employed? We cannot conceive of an intelligent and devout patriarch, or subject of patriarchal government, who would not regard the patriarchal authority as given for the glory of God, in the patronage of "good works" of a religious, as well as of a common moral cha-

Christian religion enjoins towards God and man,") &c. Guyse in loco.

racter. And finally, God himself gave a government to his own chosen Israel, and in defining its powers and functions, leaves no doubt that all the "good works" to which this government was not to be "a terror," were works such as have been specified above as those, in part, intended by Paul. In short, there is every reason—the phrase itself—the ends of the institution of government—its history and the direct teachings of the Most High in the institutes given to Israel—to believe that among the works here meant are those that come under the head of religion—religion in its exterior manifestations.

Now, to such, "rulers are not a terror." Such rulers as Paul refers to will so legislate, so judge, so apply law, as that not only the upright and peaceable, but the fearers of God and the servants of Christ, will be subject to no hinderance, exposed to no danger from the civil arm, in their Christian profession and efforts: such rulers will so act as that Christ may be preached, his law defended, his authority maintained, his church propagated, without fear of offending "the powers that be."

3. These rulers use their powers for the restraint of evil—"*but 'a terror to the evil.'*" To ascertain the import of the term "evil," we have only to institute a contrast between this clause and the pre-

ceding. "Good works" are such works as are appropriate to the honest, peaceable, and moral. Of course, "evil works" are such as dishonesty, turbulence, theft, and all gross departures from morality. "Good works" are such as honour Christ, the Sabbath, the Scriptures, and the name and supreme dignity of a Three-one God. "Evil" works are such as are adverse to all these—blasphemy, profanity, idolatry, and Sabbath violation. Can it be possible that an inspired apostle could use this term in any narrower sense, particularly in defining a divine ordinance?

To all these the rulers here meant are for a "terror." They enact such laws, and so administer these enactments, as that all disorder, vice, and open disregard to God and religion may be discountenanced, and, when circumstances demand this, restrained.

Here, again, we may appeal to collateral sources of argument, to the uniform testimony of the Word of God, and to the examples of all enlightened nations. To the former we need only refer. From the patriarchal ages onward until the canon of Old Testament revelation—none can doubt that divinely approved civil governments, and acts of civil rulers, are of this character—a "terror to evil works;" and in the New, so far as this aspect of national institutions is referred to, we have but the continuation of the same teachings. "The law," says Paul—meaning, in part, at least, the law of God as established among the Jews—"is not made for a righteous man, but for the lawless and disobedient, for the ungodly and for sinners," &c.; and "if there be any other thing that is contrary to sound doctrine." (1 Tim. i. 9–10.) Nor has any Christian nation found itself able fully to reduce to practice any other theory. In words, many do, indeed, deny that acts injurious to morality even, and more, that acts hurtful to religion, can rightfully become subjects of cognizance by the magistrate; but just so far as Christian principle has made itself felt, either directly or by tradition, among any people, have they been obliged to conform to the apostle's definition; very defectively it is true, in most instances, but still sufficiently to show that Christian sense and a regard for the general welfare of society, will not be satisfied without some acknowledgment of the principle. Hence, the laws by which the Sabbath is guarded —laws against shameful vices—laws against blasphemy and profanity—or to present the same fact in a more general and more striking form, where is the government that would think itself justifiable in guarding against the spread of acknowledged moral good, as they do of moral evil?

Nor does it weaken the force of our argument, drawn from the practice of nations, that the legislation to which we have referred is affirmed to be only an indirect way of answering what some call the only end of civil rule—the preservation of peace and of property. At all events, it is admitted to be *necessary:* and if necessary, there can be no question whatever that this sort of governmental action was contemplated in the institution itself. So far as our present purpose is concerned, this is enough; for Paul, certainly, did not intend to omit, in his definition of the functions of rulers, a class of acts without which they cannot carry on a permanently wholesome administration of affairs.

On every ground, then, we maintain that Paul designs, in these phrases, to furnish us with a summary, but very comprehensive, view of the official character of such rulers as may lawfully claim our conscientious allegiance and subjection. They are such as render themselves "a terror" not to "good works," in any sound sense, but "to the evil" in every sense in which *outward* acts are so. Such are the "powers" whom "God has ordained;" such he owns as his "ministers;" the resistance offered to these offends him. All this we will find amply confirmed by the Apostle himself when he proceeds, immediately, to apply the general statement to the different classes of citizens in the State, to the good and the bad.*

SECTION IV.

THE APPLICATION OF THESE PRINCIPLES TO THE CASE BOTH OF GOOD AND BAD CITIZENS.

"Wilt thou then not be afraid of the power? Do that which is good, and thou wilt have praise of the same; for he is the minister of God to thee for good. But if thou do that which is evil, be afraid; for he beareth not the sword in vain, for he is the minister of God, a revenger to execute wrath upon him that doeth evil." Verses 3 and 4.

IN these clauses Paul applies, and, in so doing, more fully illustrates, the doctrines previously taught in regard to the functions of the civil magistrate. He makes this application:

First, to the case of the upright and faithful citizen. And

1. *Good conduct will secure certain advantages under such a government as he has described.* V. 3, "Wilt thou then not be afraid of the power? Do that which is good, and thou shalt have praise of the same." The first clause seems to be intended to meet an objection; an objection to this

---

* Inferences will be deduced from this section, in connexion with those of the subsequent section.

effect: Civil government is armed with terror—it
addresses itself to the fears of men—and, hence,
it is inconsistent for a Christian to regard it at all.
"Well," says Paul, "Wilt thou not be afraid?"
Dost thou wish not to be afraid? "Do that which
is good," and you need cherish no fear. The law,
as armed with penal sanctions, "is not for the
righteous man." (1 Tim. i. 9.) Such, by the
grace of God enlightening and guiding them, are
a law to themselves, &c., hence may live, and do
live, under just civil rule without fear, at least,
without slavish fear—without any such fear as is
adverse to unalloyed Christian peace.

And even more, "Do that which is good, *and
thou shalt have praise of the same.*" It is not, of
course, to be inferred, from this language, that
civil government is instituted for the purpose of
conferring rewards, in any gross form, upon even
the best citizens: still good conduct secures praise;
for by an upright, peaceable and Christian deportment, good citizens acquire reputation and influence, and, in such a government as Paul describes,
this class of citizens, and this only, would be admitted to places of power and trust. These are
no mean rewards. It is no inconsiderable result
of becoming conduct, that it attracts the favourable
regard of the community, and opens the way to
seats of more eminent influence.

2. This the Apostle proceeds *to confirm*. V. 4.
"For he is the minister of God to thee for good."

We have here a two-fold argument—one drawn
from the relation which the magistrate bears to
God, another from the end of his appointment.

(1.) *The magistrate is God's servant.* "For he
is the minister (διακονος) of God;" and that in a
sense, not materially different from that in which
ministers are styled (διακονοι) "servants of
Christ." They are so, inasmuch as they administer a divinely appointed ecclesiastical constitution, and perform, in Christ's name, duties which
he has prescribed, and this for the attainment of
ends clearly expressed in the laws pertaining to
the church's organization. So civil rulers; for
they, also, are called to administer a divine institution for the promotion of the ends contemplated
in the ordinance of civil society: the parallel
holds in another most important particular.
The servant of Christ is, necessarily, under law
to Christ, not only as accountable to Him for the
manner in which his service is performed, but as
the very performance itself is regulated by laws
which Christ, his Master, has enacted. So, with
some limitations, we assert of the civil ruler. He
is not, indeed, furnished with a complete code of
laws, but he has sufficiently clear intimations, par-

ticularly with the Bible before him, of the will of his Master: he is to be "a terror, not to good works, but to the evil." And now the parallel ought surely to hold in another respect.—Who will say that that man is a "servant of Christ," even although he occupy the seat, and professes to act in that character, no matter how many acknowledge him, who disregards the law of Christ, perverts the gospel, and tramples on the rights of his people? What Protestant, for example, acknowledges the Pope of Rome as a "servant of Christ?" And yet he has his millions of votaries, and claims to be Christ's vicegerent. *He* is "a servant of Christ," who *serves* Christ. So, in the case of civil rule. How can he be the servant of God, in administering civil rule, who either denies God's supremacy, or perverts the ends of government, and, particularly, if he also employ his power against God, his law, his gospel, his church and his Son.*

But, to return. The magistrate is "God's servant," and, hence, it *must* be the end and

* It is one objection to this that Cyrus is called God's shepherd. (Is. xliv. 28.) This refers merely to the fact that Cyrus was raised up for a particular purpose. The devil is, in the same providential sense, Christ's servant.

design of his office to do God's work. God is his Master, whose law, gospel, glory and kingdom the magistrate must seek to promote: as God is a praise to them that do well, so must the ruler be also, for he is called to act as his servant.

(2.) The magistrate is God's servant for the good of God's people. "The minister of God to thee for good." "To thee!" To whom? To every citizen, certainly. The design of the appointment of civil rulers is, that they may be useful—that they may be employed in securing the rights, the liberty, the safety, the property, of every citizen. As previously remarked, "the civil authority extends its ægis over every person and every interest in the commonwealth." Are we at liberty to exclude the Christian citizen? Assuredly not. Indeed, Paul seems to refer with peculiar emphasis to the godly. To them he addresses this epistle. By what right, then, does any one undertake to say, that, in this phrase, Paul alludes only to the citizen, and that, merely in reference to his common social rights? Every rule of interpretation forbids this. We do not affirm that he means the church alone—not even the church directly—but we are assured that it is "handling the word of God" most unfairly, to exclude the church and the faithful in their character as servants of Christ. And can we conceive it possible that God has set up such an institution, armed with such powers, and yet has done this, without any regard to the safety, the assistance of his own friends, the disciples of his Son, in that great work to which they have been especially and imperatively called? This is impossible: the thought is dishonouring to God. The magistrate is set up that he may guard the rights of every member of the community—protect the weak against the strong—restrain all violence—promote every good work, and so secure the welfare of the whole community; but surely, as God's "servant," he must have a special concern for the name, and cause, and kingdom of God, as these are, in a still higher sense, intrusted to the faithful, and exemplified in them.

But, is this all? Has the "minister of God" fulfilled his whole functions, when he merely secures the religious liberties of the faithful? He has not. He is a "minister for *good*." As God's servant to do his work, he must seek, by some positive acts, the "good" of the friends of God. He must be, in this sense, "a praise" to them that do well. He must give them encouragement and sustain them in their Christian efforts. In a word, he must copy the example of the patriarchs;

for, as we have already seen, this was required of *them*. He must copy the example of godly rulers in Israel—as far as the general principle is concerned, for this was required imperatively of them. He must not fall behind even heathen kings, who, like Cyrus, passed decrees and promoted their execution, for the re-building of Jerusalem and the establishment of God's worship.

2. Paul applies the doctrine respecting the ends of government *to the case of bad citizens.* V. 4. "But if thou do that which is evil, be afraid : for he beareth not the sword in vain : for he is the minister of God, a revenger to execute wrath upon him that doeth evil."

In these clauses we have the reverse picture of the action of a right civil government. The same general arrangement is followed—

1. *The Apostle asserts that evil doers have reason to fear its power.* "But, if thou do evil, be afraid." This, no doubt, refers to such evil acts as strike directly at the authority of government, the peace of society and the property, the reputation, or the life of well disposed citizens. But, it embraces more. Unless we are prepared to limit it as neither the word of God nor the practice of enlightened nations warrants, it must be interpreted in a wider sense, so as to include acts com-

mitted against the laws of morality—such as profanity, blasphemy, and open dishonour done to God and his Christ—to such as commit these the faithful ruler is a "terror;" they may justly fear him. This statement Paul,

2. In the second place, confirms : for (1.) *The magistrate is invested with punitive power.* "He beareth the sword." This language is partially figurative. The "sword" is the emblem of the power of civil government to inflict pains and penalties. In this respect, civil authority stands in direct and striking contrast to ecclesiastical; for the latter has no other power than that which appeals to the understanding, the heart and the conscience : it can act by means of admonition, reproof, exhortation, and, in the last resort, can place the erroneous and the immoral outside the pale of the visible church. Civil authority sustains itself and enforces its enactments by penalties of a different sort, when necessary. It uses force, not as the only means of securing conformity to its decrees, for it also may use admonition and persuasion—but, as the last resort, when milder measures fail.

The "sword," moreover, is an instrument of death—for, so far as this even may the magistrate go, in the punishment of signal crimes, either

against the State or its citizens. Still, we are
not to infer that every crime is to be punished
with this extreme penalty. Far from it. The
"sword" here is, we repeat, an emblem,—the
power of the sword comprehending every grade
of penal infliction, from the smallest fine to the
severest sort of punishment. Civil rulers are endowed with power to affix and execute suitable
penal sanctions.

(2.) *Rulers, such as Paul here intends, will, in
this respect, do their duty.* "He beareth not the
sword in vain." The righteous magistrate, who
knows his place, and has a proper sense of the
nature and functions of the magistracy, will not
allow the transgressors of law to escape with im-
punity. He not only "bears the sword"—he is
not only armed with a just authority—he will use
the "sword:" it will not lie idly in the scabbard;
he will exercise the power with which he has been
invested. Faithful to his calling and to the great
interests of social and moral order, the upright
civil functionary, whether in a higher or an inferior station, will not permit God's authority to be
impugned, or the interests of society to suffer, from
unrestrained lawlessness—from flagrant breaches of
the peace—from rampant immorality—from gross,
avowed and open hostility to the name and law of

God. To be indifferent to these, or to administer law partially, inflicting punishment upon the weak and unprotected, while the evil deeds of the elevated and strong are winked at, is a virtual abdication of power. Such may "bear the sword," but they bear it "in vain." They are no more rulers, as Paul speaks of them, than he is a soldier who neglects or refuses to draw his sword in the heat of the conflict: they inspire no "terror;" evil is put under no salutary restraints, "evil" in its worst forms, at least. In short, the magistrate who can claim the subjection here enjoined is no idler; he *acts*, even in this, the most trying department of his office; for

(3.) "*He is the minister of God.*" So Paul has already, in the first clause of this verse, styled the magistrate, but in a different connexion—in a different aspect of his functions. Then he considered him as engaged in ministering to the welfare of the good and honest, particularly Christian citizens—here as the minister of God in another aspect, and yet not in any materially different sense. God is good. He is a beneficial sovereign. He has established institutions among men for the good of man; and committed their administration to the hands of men. So far as they come up to the standard, these institutions,

6*

in their actual operation, exercise a salutary influence over all who subject themselves to their sway and direction. But God is also just—a righteous law-giver. The divine government gives no countenance to sin : it is ever against it. And, hence, the Most High has invested all his institutions with some kind and degree of restraining power; and has given them laws by which they are to be guided in the disciplinary or punitive department of their functions. In this sense, parents are "ministers of God," in the training of their children—church officers in the exercise of discipline, and, now, we add, civil rulers in the inflictions of penal law. "Servants of God;" for they act by his authority, and are limited and directed by his supreme and sovereign enactments.

But why does Paul introduce this here? Partly to justify the penal administration of law, partly to gain due respect for the magistrate in this responsible and difficult part of his magistratical calling, and partly to confirm the preceding statement, that the magistracy of which he treats will not allow the wicked to pass unnoticed and unrebuked. How can he be, "for he is the minister of God" for good to man. He is also

(4.) "*A revenger—to execute wrath upon him that doeth evil.*" Εκδικος--a revenger, or more properly, an "avenger:" for the vindication of law, in its excellence, authority and obligation, is not "revenge," in the sense commonly affixed to that term. Nor does the word properly import this. When Paul speaks of the magistrate as an "avenger," it is in view of the fact that the end of penal sanctions is eminently vindicatory. In this, the civil magistrate is the "minister of God" to whom "vengeance belongs" in its highest and most ample sense—for "He will repay." He has, however, invested the magistrate with a portion, so to speak—a small portion, indeed—of His own ineffable supremacy and power, that he may employ it as His "servant" in the maintenance of the high claims of equity, truth, peace and purity in the commonwealth; and, that, if called for, he may present before the eyes of the subject or the citizen, examples of the inflexible demands of that law which is "holy" and "just" as well as "good."

If these views be correct, it appears to follow very plainly, that the "wrath" which the magistrate administers implies no *passion* of resentment in the mind of the ruler. This need have no place—in all ordinary cases ought to have none. Remembering the ultimate source of his power, the God-fearing judge or executive officer will calmly, and with no desire of personal vengeance, apply to offenders the punishment which their crimes have *merited*.

The sum of this entire section is—that such magistrates as Paul here means will not be remiss, either in protecting, and fostering the good, or in punishing the bad. They may not, they will not, be perfect. Parents, the best, are not. Ecclesiastical rulers are not. Neither can we look for perfection in civil functionaries. But at these objects good rulers will aim.

INFERENCES.

1. *It is evident that the apostle enjoins subjection only to such governments as answer the ends of the institution of magistracy.* Great injustice is done to this passage by regarding it in any other way than as a whole. Separate the first and second verses from the context, and they seem to inculcate a blind and complete submission to any authority that may happen to exist. Study the entire passage, and we learn just the contrary.—That the constitution and laws and magistrates here meant by the "higher" powers, are such as have for their object the well-being of society, and the glory of God, appears from the connexion between the clauses we have now sought to explain, and the apostle's injunction of obedience. " Be subject—

for rulers are not a terror," &c. Otherwise, we must lay to Paul's charge, and to the charge of the Spirit, by whom he was directed, the singular assertion, that every government that can possibly exist is "a praise to them that do well," as Rome, Austria, France! The governments of these countries are all a praise to them that do well—no "terror" these to good works! The truth is, as has been urged before, no reference is made whatever to bad governments or bad magistrates. We here again refer to the great champion of the friends of liberty as against high prerogative in England, from whom we have already quoted pretty largely. "We may judge, from what I have said, how little ground there is, from any thing here delivered by Paul, to argue to so unlimited a submission as some inculcate. For we see he hath his eye all the way upon the end of all government, and founds his precepts upon this supposition that the rulers answer that good end. If they do not, or if they set themselves to contradict it by oppression, violence, and injustice; by invading and destroying the public happiness, and by bringing on public miseries; the apostle seems not to think of recommending submission to the subject. For whilst he commands submission, he puts no case of princes acting contrary to the purpose of their institution, and the sole business of their office, much less of princes who make an express contract with their people, and solemn oaths to preserve their rights and liberties, and afterwards break through all these ties to invade their happiness. Nor doth he mention any thing of a passive submission in such cases; but plainly leaves nations to the dictates of common sense and the powerful law of self-preservation; and this under all forms of government equally." "That governor who contradicts the character here laid down by Paul, who is not a terror to evil works, but to good; who is not a minister of good to the virtuous, but of vengeance to the wicked only; and who is not continually watching for the good and happiness of human society, is not the governor whom Paul means in this place, or to whom he here presseth obedience. Can any one deny that governors are thus described in this place? or that those governors, which are here described, are the governors whom Paul here means? or that this description of his is the argument from whence he presseth subjection in point of conscience? and doth it not follow manifestly from hence, That the governor who contradicts all this description is not the governor here described, and, consequently, not the governor to whom he here presseth obedience? Had it been

Paul's design to press obedience to the greatest tyrants and oppressors; or had he had in his eye any particular emperor, who was a monster, not only of villany, but of public oppression (as some represent his sense;) nothing can be imagined more unaccountable than that he should give such a description of governors as to exclude those whom there was most occasion to mention, and that he should reason Christians into a conscientious subjection in such a manner, as cannot conclude for subjection to any but such governors as he describes in the foregoing words, and as come up to that sense of them in which they should be understood. And if any one can prove that it is possible he should intend by governors who are continually attending to the good of their subjects, not only such but also governors who are continually attending and watching to make their subjects miserable; and if any one can show me the conclusiveness of this argument, rulers are by their office obliged to be a terror to evil works, and not to the good; therefore you are obliged in conscience to submit to them, when they are a terror to good works; then I will retract this sentence.''*

* Hoadly, pp. 9, 21, 22. It is but just to state that Hoadly does not *directly* extend the "good works" and the "evil" so far as we have done. With this exception,

2. *Civil government should extend its protection to every class, and particularly to the more feeble.* It should be a "praise" to all that do well—a "terror" to all that do ill. Indeed, nothing can be more certain than that the defence of the poor, of the weak, was one chief object in ordaining civil authority. Surely, it was never contemplated in the divine arrangements in reference to the exercise of civil rule, that it should become, in his name, the instrument of establishing and protecting violence and wrong—in defending the strong in their avaricious, cruel oppression of the destitute and the helpless. That civil rulers can prevent all wrong, we are far from affirming—but this they should aim at. If they do the reverse—if they throw their shield over him who deprives his fellow of his rights and liberties, or spoils him of his property—in short, if they sanction such systems as those of serfage and slavery, or even of political oppression, they are not the rulers here designated. And more than this, and still more plainly, if a government deliberately incorporate, among the principles of its constitution, such wrongs, how can

his exposition agrees with ours. As to the above principle, he goes as far as we do, utterly denying that the mere existence of a government entitles it to obedience.

it be the ordinance of God for good—or its rulers "ministers of God for good," as Paul here so emphatically styles them? The victims of the wrong may be few comparatively,—they may belong to despised races, but no matter—the government that gives its sanction, knowingly, to injustice— that tolerates so heinous a sin and crime, cannot claim a place among those here meant. It may be free, in other respects—it may allow unlimited scope to the plans and efforts of the *favoured* class; it may be endowed with many attractive features; but if it be the patron of the enslavers of men—if they are crowned with its honours, while the subjects of their ambition, pride, avarice or cruelty, are cast out of the pale of law—and is not this the case even in this land?—such a government stands here condemned.

3. *That many, at least, of the existing governments of the world, have no claim to conscientious acknowledgment.* Try Austria. Is it the good, the God-fearing, the disciples of Christ, that gain for themselves a good name and influence in that Empire? Does the Austrian government prove "a terror" to the immoral, the profane, the impious? These inquiries bear with them, in the mind of every intelligent man, their own answers. True, even Austria does not employ its coercive

7

power against every thing good. It permits industry and common honesty, and will restrain the robber and the cheat. But, on the other hand, does it not forbid the free circulation of the scriptures? Does it not discountenance and prove itself "a terror" to pure religion? Does it not exert a power, professedly from God, to prevent the diffusion of genuine Christianity? As all know, this iniquitous government lays its hand upon education, upon the church, upon the Bible; it banishes missionaries, it builds up its highest barriers against efforts to bring its millions of ignorant and deluded subjects to the knowledge of "the truth as it is in Jesus." And, still more, its great aim is to prevent free thought, free speech, and the free circulation of intelligence; and it labours, with all authority, to keep down the masses, and subject them to the control of a corrupt and pampered aristocracy. Were Paul—were Christ himself to appear among them, and teach as they taught, bonds, imprisonment and death would await them. In a word, is it the pious, the devout, the energetic Christian to whom this despotic power becomes "a praise?" Nothing of the kind.

How is it with France? The reply is but the repetition of our account of Austria. Famous, indeed, has France been, whether as kingdom, republic, or empire, for its rejection of Christ, its hatred of his people, its persecutions of the faithful.* And so, Spain, Portugal, Tuscany, Rome, Russia, and others.

These considerations derive no little weight from the circumstance that it is not mere "submission" that is here enjoined—it is active obedience and support. Whatever government Paul means—he demands that it be not merely an outward conformity to its will—but a hearty, conscientious acknowledgment of its claims. Now, surely, the Lord does not demand that we should recognise even these governments as his "ordinance"—give them an active homage, and pay them that reverence that is due to his "ministers!" Do not all the friends of liberty earnestly desire their downfall; and all the Christian friends of liberty pray for it? Paul meant no such government. It is ridiculous to attempt to apply his description to such conspiracies against God and man as the governments we have specified, and similar ones, are. They have no place to stand on in this passage— they are "found wanting"—they cannot claim the conscientious obedience of the subjects—they, ene-

* The present government is no exception. Protestants are not, indeed, put to death, but they are discountenanced, and the circulation of the Scriptures restrained.

mies of God and of man, can impress no sanction, which God will recognise, upon their enactments.

4. *Civil government is instituted for the promotion of moral, as well as social order, among men.* That one, and a leading end of civil government, is to guard the rights of the people; in other words, that it is designed, not for the rulers, but the ruled, none will, probably, be now disposed to question. It is not so generally admitted—by many it is expressly denied—that this institution of God has any thing to do directly with morals or religion. Few are willing, indeed, to go so far as to dispute the existence of, at least, an indirect power in society to cherish the interests of morality—and, perhaps, it would be admitted that religion should receive more countenance than irreligion. But this passage proves more than this. It proves—we think it demonstrates—that there is a direct and specific obligation lying upon civil rulers to have an eye to every thing that goes to promote the glory of God, the fountain of all power, and the author of civil rule. They are not only to refrain from every thing that would interfere with pure religion and scriptural morality, but to promote well doing—to be "a praise to them that do well;" and "a terror" to all evil doers. Nor can it be fairly objected that this would issue

in persecution. It is to be remembered that the law of God is their rule, and that, in the exercise of their power, they must be limited by its pre-scriptions. Unless that law warrants persecution, rulers cannot persecute; and, besides, it remains with the objector to show how the patronage of true religion, and the restraint of that which is dishonouring to God and hurtful to his kingdom, can be denominated persecution.

5. *Civil rulers are under imperative obligations to recognise the divine supremacy, and that in their official character.* Paul here styles them the "ministers of God"—God's servants. The servant should know his master even among men. And still more should he who professes to wield an authority derived from God, in administering an "ordinance of God," acknowledge, reverence and give due homage to his sovereign. This acknowledgment should be practical. It does not consist in a mere profession of belief in His being, or even in His providence. It implies the study of his will, and a constant aim and effort to please Him. The ruler, or the nation, that claims to be above all other authority, demanding an unquestioning obedience to mere human law—that denies the existence of a "higher law," is in rebellion against God—is not a "servant," in Paul's sense. And

7*

more than this, the acknowledgment must be direct, and in express terms—it must be an acknowledgment—among enlightened people—of the supremacy of the Most High; of his laws, as the Scriptures teach them. Further, still, this acknowledgment must be rendered, not to the God of the deist—but to the only true God—the Christian's God—to God in Christ.

Does the refusal to acknowledge God invalidate the authority of a government as tyranny does? Why not? Surely, if God has ordained this institution for his glory—if he has put it under his law—if he has designed to exhibit in it something of his own majesty, ("I said that ye are gods;" Ps. lxxxii.) it is difficult to see how a government that denies the Maker and Lord of all—or withholds from him, from his law, and from his Son, even an acknowledgment, can claim his sanction upon its acts? Surely, God does not threaten with "damnation" those who refuse to bow their consciences before his enemies!*

6. *It follows, indisputably, from the whole tenor of verses 3 and 4, that civil rulers should be God-fearing men.* Every clause demonstrates this. If a ruler should be a "terror" to evil works,

* This subject, and kindred ones, will be taken up in a subsequent section.

and a "praise to them that do well"—if the magistrate is "a minister of God"—if he is under law to God in his official doings—if his duties are most onerous and responsible, involving the highest interests and dearest rights of the citizen—if his magistratical acts bear, with no little directness and force, upon the interests of morality and religion, surely, rulers should be men of principle, of integrity, of Christian character. There is, in fact, something monstrous in the idea of committing the administration of an eminent divine institution to the hands of the immoral and irreligious: and, if this be done by the vote of the people, can it be otherwise than offensive to the supreme moral Governor? On this point, also, we have the most explicit testimony of God himself: "Moreover, thou shalt provide out of the people able men— such as fear God—men of truth, hating covetousness." (Ex. xviii. 21.) "He that ruleth over men must be just, ruling in the fear of God." (2 Sam. xxiii. 3.)

Nor can it be objected that these are Old Testament injunctions. The last is a general statement; equally true—equally obligatory, in all ages. And, though the first was a law addressed to Israel in the wilderness, it is no less binding now than then. It is a declaration of the will of

God in the matter to which it relates. No reason
can be assigned why it should be regarded as now
set aside. Surely, the clearer light which the
New Testament sheds upon the things of God,
does not diminish either the duty or the necessity
of appointing to office none but such as may be
expected to honour the supreme law and moral
Governor—who will pay due regard to the heaven-
ordained ends, laws and relations of civil government. Moreover, this law is characterized by
divine wisdom. How can it be hoped that the
immoral or the irreligious will faithfully administer law? Will such men regard their oaths?
The safety of the community demands that the
power of legislating, and of judging, and of enforcing law, should be kept out of the hands of
the personally ungodly and impure. And, finally,
there is no little stress to be laid upon the matter
of example. We again quote Hoadly: "To all
other qualifications there must be joined a blame-
less example. The reason is, because every thing
that tends to promote religion and happiness in a
society, is the concern of all who have authority
in it. Now, it is with those who are to punish
vice and protect virtue, just as it is with those
who are to teach the practice of virtue, and the
abhorrence of vice. It is an observation, easy

and obvious to every body, that those who are the preachers of righteousness do no great service to the cause; but, perhaps, the contrary, if their examples, unhappily, contradict their precepts. And it is certainly the same with respect to those whose business it is to punish vice. If, whilst they punish it in inferiors, they themselves are known to be guilty of it, the correction, indeed, may make the offender avoid the light; but it will never make him in love with virtue. He will be apt to think he is punished only because he is poor, and not considerable enough to be in office himself; and may be hardened to vice, whilst he sees men making use of their authority in punishing others only, as it were, for a screen to their own greater indulgence."

7. *Government is endowed with the right of inflicting capital punishment.* Of the ruler, it has been said, "He beareth the sword,"—an emblematic expression, but importing, also, literally, a power to take life in extreme cases.

8. *The infliction of penal sanctions by national authorities is not solely for reformation, but, also, and even primarily, for the vindication of the law.* It is not affirmed that the execution of law consists entirely in acts of a punitive character. It would be so, provided government had been esta-

blished with no other view than to protect the peaceable citizen. Such a notion is most derogatory to the magistrate and the government. The civil ruler would then be no more than a policeman, and government a system of police. Government has higher functions. It is a "praise" to them that do well. And, hence, it takes an interest in all that promotes a quiet, industrious and moral behaviour—it provides for the education of the people—it ought to interest itself in the maintenance of pure religious observances.

But, after all, there will be the lawless and the vicious, who must be encountered and kept in awe by the display of the "terrors" of justice. For such characters, and for such ends, mainly, penal sanctions are annexed to law. They serve, indeed, a useful purpose in the case even of the orderly, for none are perfectly free from disturbing passions—but their main use is to alarm those who can be addressed through no other avenue than their fears. The language of the passage before us is most explicit—the magistrate is a "revenger to execute wrath." By inflicting penalties, he exhibits the desert of transgression, and shows that law is, indeed, law—that it is no mere nerveless utterance of the supreme power, but a thing of life and of energy. Still, it needs, also, to be remembered that this vengeance of the law is far from being mere vengeance—it has, even as exercised upon the offender himself, except in the case of capital punishment, a wholesome influence—and, in all cases, it serves as an admonition to others "that they may see, and fear, and do no more wickedly."

SECTION V.

THE PRINCIPLES OF OBEDIENCE TO CIVIL RULE.

This topic has been incidentally noticed in commenting upon the duty itself; but it is made the subject of a distinct statement.

"Wherefore, ye must needs be subject, not only for wrath, but also for conscience' sake." V. 5.

1. *Obedience is to be rendered partly to avoid penal inflictions*—"for wrath's sake." It is not very material to determine whether the Apostle here refers to the "wrath of the magistrate, or of God, or of both." If to the first—and the connexion in which the term occurs seems to warrant this view—it still implies that the displeasure of God, also, rests upon him who withholds due subjection from the authorities previously described. It is more important to remark that this phrase

has been frequently applied to express that sort of submission which the slave gives to his master, or the oppressed to the power of the despot—a submission altogether forced, in which there is no heartfelt recognition. There is such a subjection to lawless authority, and such a submission may be given on this principle. Moreover, this term is appropriate enough as thus applied. But it has not this meaning here. As has been frequently stated already, Paul refers, in this passage, to no usurped, tyrannical or godless power. He speaks of but one kind of government—one sort of rulers: a government worthy of obedience—rulers who are " ministers of God."

This phrase, as we find it in the passage before us, may be regarded as referring to that class whom we have styled "bad citizens;" for they are kept under only by fear of punishment. But this is not all. The Apostle is addressing Christians—urges upon them a subjection of a different and contrasted character—" not for wrath's sake," but for higher considerations; as much as to say, whatever others may do: *they* may be prompted to conduct themselves peaceably and according to law, only from selfish reasons—but let it not be so with you ; you should have another and a better spirit. Still this cannot be the leading object in the introduction of this clause, for this interpretation leaves out of view a very important word. Paul does not barely say "not for wrath's sake"—but, "not *only* for wrath's sake"—intimating that this may be exhibited as a principle of obedience even in addressing the upright citizen. And the subsequent clause confirms this; for, he adds, "but *also* for conscience' sake." Nor does this represent the passage as urging a principle unworthy of the Christian. Subjection to lawful authority *merely* for fear is, indeed, radically defective; but such a fear is, collaterally, a lawful principle of action. Hence, in covenanting with Adam, the Most High appeals to this principle: "The day thou eatest thereof thou shalt surely die." In fact, the penalty is essential to the law in the case of all fallible creatures. It is "law" from the very fact that it is armed with such a sanction. And, besides, it must be remembered that even the best are here imperfect—that they are, in fact, under the influence of corrupt emotions and appetites, and, consequently, require the restraining influence of such considerations as those to which the inspired writer here appeals. God deals with even the faithful as subjects of discipline. He warns them of paternal displeasure in case they sin, and when they do sin, visits

8

them with his chastisements. And, finally, the Apostle here brings to view the majesty and terror of civil government, not as belonging to itself alone, but as a transcript, however faint, of the ineffable dignity and eminence of Him in whose name "the sword" is borne and used. In short, there is here presented *one*—though an inferior one—of the principles which move the citizen, or the subject, to a whole-souled obedience to the lawful commands of a lawful power. There is another; for, it is added,

2. *"But also for conscience' sake."* All know something from their own experience of the nature and workings of conscience. Philosophers may debate the question, whether it is a distinct faculty, or the result of the operation of certain faculties; but all, learned and unlearned, agree that it is through the action of conscience that man is made to *feel* his accountability to the Invisible and Supreme. It implies, if it does not essentially consist in, the possession of a moral sense; a sense which judges of right and wrong, not by any humanly enacted law, or with reference to the judgment of an earthly tribunal, but in view of a law of divine obligation and the presence of an unseen Judge. "We believe it," says McCosh, "to be an original, a divinely appointed, a funda-

mental law. Still, though persons could succeed
in analyzing it, it would not be the less a law.
Suppose there is nothing else in the mind, when
contemplating moral actions, but the springing
up of emotions, still there must be a *Heaven-
appointed* law, otherwise the emotions would not
be so invariable."

Conscience then has ever an eye, in all its judgments and dictates, to the tribunal of God. But
to what particular duty, or aspect of duty, are its
judgments directed as it is here introduced by the
apostle? An attempt has been made to connect it
with the preceding clause; as if Paul designed to
enforce a bare heartless submission, for "wrath's
sake," to an unjust or a hard governmental authority, out of conscience towards God.

Now, it is not denied that in case such submission is properly yielded, and we have admitted that
in certain instances it may be, it should be yielded
with a good conscience. The slave who plies his
labour at the bidding of even a tyrannical master,
may do this conscientiously—in part, as he regards
his condition in the light of an affliction befalling
him in the providence of God, and in part, as he
may be influenced by a respect to certain other
considerations, such as his own comfort, which
every man is bound to promote, so far as he can,
without sin, in the exemplification of a meek and

quiet spirit, even under the infliction of wrong. But to this the apostle makes no reference here. Unless we have mistaken altogether the drift of the passage, that it relates to good governors, it is impossible that he could. And, moreover, Paul does not say, "Submit for fear of punishment, out of conscience towards God:" giving, in the last clause, a reason for the injunction of the first, or a rule to guide in fulfilling it: "*but* we must needs be subject," that is under obedience, "not only for wrath's, but also for conscience' sake;" thus assigning not one reason, but two distinct ones. And, finally, this verse is clearly a conclusion from the whole of the preceding exhibition of the nature and functions of civil power. "Therefore," inasmuch as the "higher powers" are "ordained of God"—inasmuch as "rulers are a terror to the evil, but a praise to them that do well"—inasmuch as government is a divine and a beneficent institution, "ye must needs be subject for conscience' sake."

The last paragraph embodies the substance of the meaning of this clause. To obey for "conscience' sake" is to obey because God *requires* it—because the lawful magistrate is invested with a legitimate authority to administer an ordinance of God's appointment — because the judgment is "the Lord's."* And, finally, because a good government is conducive to the peace, the morality, the religious interests of society.

This is the true, as it is a high principle of obedience to civil rule. And, in fact, in the case of good citizens, it is the main reason why wholesome laws are conformed to. Such have respect, not to any mere human arrangements, but to an institution which bears the impress and sanction of God's name, law, wisdom, supremacy, and majesty. Wherever these are seen, the homage and allegiance of the godly are sincere and genuine. They yield no mere outward and constrained service. What they do as members of the commonwealth, they do "as to the Lord, and not unto men."

REMARKS.

1. *It is not left optional with men whether they support righteous civil institutions or not.* We mean as before God. That the citizen may—that he must—"prove" civil institutions and laws, has already been inferred from the preceding statements and reasonings of this passage. But having

* 2 Chron. xix. 8. Of course it is not meant that the magistrate is infallible, but he acts with God's sanction in so far as he acts rightly.

proved these and found them endowed with the attributes of God's moral ordinance of magistracy—having proved the magistrates themselves, and the design and tendencies of their administration, and approved them, he is not at liberty to withhold the outward tokens of his approval. "Conscience" has to do with it. It has to do with Him who is "Lord of the conscience."

2. *All obedience to civil authority is limited by the higher allegiance due to God its author.* To imagine otherwise is to annihilate, by the law of God, its own authority and sanctions. All right subjection to civil rule regards it as the creature of God, but *no more.* It surely does not give it God's place. Indeed nothing can be more absurd than the notion that "conscience," which always sees God as supreme in His claims and power, should, for a moment, substitute any "lower law" for His. This would be to deny its own nature—to act in direct opposition to the very law of its being. And, hence,

3. *Every attempt to establish a paramount claim for any mere human enactment is really, under the pretence of doing honour to government, to imperil the stability and efficiency of all authority.* What could any government do—unless one of mere force—without the aid and co-operation of the

principle of conscience? And what do they seek to accomplish, who deride "The Higher Law," but to sap the very foundations of the social state? Instead of being the friends, such men are the very worst enemies of civil government. Could they absorb the conscience of the individual, and deprive him of the right and the disposition to judge for himself, in the light of God's law, and supremacy, and word, they would but make a community of the very lowest order of slaves, and thus sow the seeds of inevitable disorders and revolutions. They, and they alone, are the friends of civil law and social order, who vindicate the paramount claims of the supreme Potentate, and maintain the rights of an enlightened conscience. Hence,

4. *May be ascertained the reason why the nations are so generally dissatisfied, and that the more as knowledge increases, with existing governments.* It is because they find in them so little that bears the stamp of rectitude of aim; so little that bears the impress of the divine majesty. True, there are the lawless—the vicious—who, under any administration, would require the exercise of a restraining hand. The discontent we refer to is not only of such. It is that of the thoughtful, the intelligent, the benevolent, the devout. Their dissatisfaction may not always make itself manifest, but it is not

the less real. It appears in the withdrawing of
many good men from all active concern in politics,
and in the longing of the pious for the coming of
a time when iniquity shall no longer find refuge
under the wings of power—when the legislators
and executive officers of the nations shall be trust-
worthy men—when the entire workings of the
social fabric shall be eminently conducive to the
promotion of individual and national weal. It
will be well for the world when civil government
shall be avowedly restored to the domain of conscience—conscience toward God, His law, His
Christ, and His gospel.

SECTION VI.

A SPECIFIC STATEMENT OF THE DUTIES OF SUB-
JECTS AND CITIZENS.

THUS far the duty of subjection has been stated
in general terms, and pressed upon general considerations. The apostle now proceeds more in
detail.

1. The requisite contributions are to be made
for the maintenance of government.

*"For, for this cause pay ye tribute also: for they are
God's ministers, attending continually upon this very thing."*
Verse 6.

The word here rendered "tribute" (φορους) signifies, literally—as does our word by which it is rendered—the contributions levied upon a conquered state or province. It also means any direct tax laid indiscriminately upon all citizens—such as land tax, capitation tax, or a tax upon personal estate; and, even more generally, any kind of levy by which national revenues are gathered, with the exception of customs. This is its meaning here, and the payment of such taxes is enforced by a three-fold argument—and, (1.) From the nature, and ends, and benefits of civil rule. "For this cause pay ye tribute." Some expositors regard this clause as referring to the preceding verse, and, consequently, as urging a conscientious response to the pecuniary demands of government. To this interpretation there can be no doctrinal objection. This is, in fact, the very gist of the precept contained in the entire verse. It is better, however, to consider this clause as looking back to the whole of the foregoing teachings of the apostle on the subject of civil power and its exercise, with special reference to the great argument which lies at the foundation of the general duty of subjection— the fact that civil government is no mere human arrangement, but a divine institution. (2.) The apostle argues from the fact that magistrates are God's "ministers." That they are so, has been previously stated, and the import of the term we have attempted to explain, viz., that it designates civil rulers as the servants of God, not in the general way in which all things, even inanimate, serve Him, inasmuch as they are controlled by His power, and guided by His hand, so that they are instruments of accomplishing his unalterable purposes; but in a limited and specific sense, as they are employed in administering his law, in administering authority which He has ordained, in executing functions which he has prescribed. In other words, magistrates are God's "ministers," in a sense analogous to that in which ecclesiastical functionaries are "ministers" of Christ. This view is clearly expressed by the term here rendered "ministers." It is not the same with that used in the fourth verse. There it is " διακονος," here it is "λειτουργοι"—a title given by the Athenians to those employed by the state in particular offices by national appointment, and often used by the inspired writers in the sense of holding a public office or ministry. In Heb. x. 11, it denotes the exercise of the priestly office. The occupant of civil power—by whatever form of lawful procedure invested with power—is still the "minister" of

God. To withhold such contributions as the exigencies of the government require, is, consequently, a dishonour done to God, by whom the magistrate has been appointed and his duties assigned. (3.) The payment of taxes is a duty inasmuch as they are justly due—due upon the principle of work done, and benefit conferred. "Attending continually upon this very thing." Not the collection of taxes merely. It is impossible that this can be the apostle's meaning. Civil rulers are not *mere* tax gatherers. And those who are specially employed in this department are principally of that class to whom, least of all, the passage refers. The magistracy—a good magistracy, and the apostle speaks of no other—"attend" to higher duties, to the advancement of the public weal, the promotion of peace, of social and moral order, of religion, of the glory of God. On this ground, then, it becomes a duty to contribute conscientiously to the national funds. There is a service rendered—a work done —benefit received; and on the common principles of equity which regulate all matters of a pecuniary kind in common intercourse and business.

It may be regarded as strange that this—as we would probably regard it — inferior civil duty should thus be made to occupy the first place in the detailed exhibition of what is comprehended in "subjection" to the "higher powers." Further reflection shows the wisdom of this arrangement; for while the moral and industrious—good citizens —and such are here mainly addressed, though the duty of all is taught—will not be easily drawn into any course of conduct adverse to social order, it is by no means so easy, even for such, to bear in mind the fact that taxes are to be conscientiously paid—that to defraud the public revenues, directly or indirectly, is to sin against God—not only on the ground and for the reason that it is sin to withhold from any what is their due, but also for the specific reason that the magistrate is God's "minister," and that thence it is a kind of sacrilege to refuse to contribute to the public treasury.

Having, for some such reason as we have assigned, presented this duty, separately and distinctly, Paul proceeds,

2. *To present, in one view, the whole range of duties owing to civil rulers.*

"Render, therefore, to all their dues; tribute to whom tribute; custom to whom custom; fear to whom fear; honour to whom honour." Verse 7.

The subject is still that of civil rule, and, hence, the first clause, which in its terms admits of a wider extension, is limited to the general subject of the passage: "Render to all" in authority "their dues;" for among the "higher powers" some are employed particularly in one department, and some in another. Let each receive that sort of subjection which his peculiar place renders especially imperative. And,

(1.) As before, "Tribute to whom tribute." (2.) "Custom to whom custom." The rendering here is literal and exact. The word used by the apostle (τελος) has precisely the signification here given it. It denotes that sort of revenues which is gathered by impost laid upon property imported from other nations—as tribute (φορος) comprehends all kinds of revenues raised within the national boundaries. (3.) "Fear to whom fear;" meaning not a slavish fear, but that awe which a righteous administration of power is designed and calculated to awaken in the mind of the subject of civil rule; such an awe as leads to a quiet and orderly obedience to the law and its appointed judges and executors. (4.) "Honour to whom honour;" for the magistrate, worthy of the name, deserves, "for his work's sake," as occupying a high place as God's "minister," a peculiar esteem, regard, and homage. His person should be treated with respect, and his faithful administration of law should secure to him the unfeigned respect of the citizen and the Christian. And this, not only for his office' sake, or his

9

work's sake, but as essential to the due influence of his authority in the restraint of the disobedient and the lawless. For, if "honour" be not paid him—if his attempts to vindicate just law, and to advance the public interests, be not sustained by the good opinion of the order-loving portion of the community—if they indulge in contempt of his person, it is evident his authority will be little feared by that class of the population which especially requires the control of sound legislative and judicial action. It was a precept of heavenly wisdom, "Thou shalt not speak evil of the ruler of thy people."

We have said the magistrate "worthy of the name;" for neither reason nor scripture demands or even justifies the rendering of honour to the tyrannical, the immoral, the profane, the godless. Reason does not; for this would tend to confound all moral distinction. To honour the undeserving is contrary to every right feeling—to every intelligent conviction; for what claim to "honour," as "the minister of God," has one like the present Emperor of France—a licentious, godless adventurer, elected by craft and violence to his seat of power; or a Pius IX. the occupant of a blasphemous throne—the deceiver and oppressor of his ruined States—the prime leader in Satan's grand array against Christ and his gospel? Such may wear the crown—they may shine in purple or in scarlet—they may receive the homage of the pliant and interested tools of their base conspiracies against God and man,—but right reason forbids us to regard them with that "honour" which the power "ordained of God" may justly demand.

The Scriptures most clearly sanction what in this matter reason teaches. Saul was King of Israel; but, at the same time, he was a rebel against God; and Samuel, the Lord's prophet, thus addressed him, "I will not return to thee; for thou hast rejected the word of the Lord, and the Lord hath rejected thee from being king over Israel." (1 Sam. xv. 26.) And Elisha, born within the limits of the ten tribes, not only withheld all tokens of "honour" from their idolatrous king, Ahab, but publicly denounced him as unworthy of the notice of the Lord's prophet: "As the Lord of hosts liveth, before whom I stand, surely, were it not that I regard the presence of Jehoshaphat the King of Judah, I would not look towards thee, nor see thee." (2 Kings iii. 14.) And our Lord himself, speaking of Herod, says, "Go ye, and tell that *fox*, Behold, I cast out devils, and I do cures to-day and to-morrow, and the third day I shall be perfected." (Luke xiii. 32.)

"Honour" is too precious to be lavished upon the base, the godless, the cruel.

REMARKS.

1. *Common, every-day duties are to be performed religiously.*—This is clearly implied in the whole strain of the verses before us. They embrace the discharge of *all* civil duties, the whole subject of obedience to the law; and the motives by which these are enforced are, throughout, religious. That is not true religion whose practical influence extends no farther than acts of devotion, or to relations merely domestic and ecclesiastical. Genuine piety and godliness are all-pervading. The *heart* of the truly devout is, in every principle, in every emotion, in every purpose, quickened and renovated by a new and energetic life; a life possessed of such properties as necessarily constitute it a universal principle of action. "If any man be in Christ, he is a new creature—old things are passed away; behold, *all things are* become new," (2 Cor. v. 17.) Hence, even the making of pecuniary contributions for the maintenance of government, is an act to be performed with an eye to the law and authority of God, as the *prime* consideration. That sort of religion which confines its guiding and restraining influence to *any* limited

sphere should not merely be suspected but denounced. The sincere Christian will be a Christian in the mart of business, in the hall of legislation, in the seat of science, in the executive chair, and in the walks of social intercourse. He stands ever in direct contrast with the godless—for "God *is* in all his thoughts," and he is bound by, and *ought* to feel the obligations of the divine law and the responsibilities of the Christian character, in every place, relation, and act,—and can, of course, no more sanction or do any thing to sustain error, heresy, or wrong, blasphemy, idolatry, or oppression, Socinianism, popery, or slaveholding, when employed in civil or political functions, than in the family, the sanctuary, or the court of ecclesiastical judicature. Hence,

2. *It is equally clear that all civil duties are to be done with reference to Christ as the administrator of the law of Heaven.*—It is admitted that the passage before us makes no direct allusion to Christ as the medium of all true and acceptable obedience to God. But this is not the less implied. If magistrates are to be "feared" and "honoured" devoutly and religiously, it must be in Christ. Moreover, we may and ought to compare Scripture with Scripture. One passage—as this—enjoins duties, and states the general principles on which

9*

they are to be performed: other passages exhibit the precise form in which the service is to be rendered. Turning to these we find their light and teaching clear and explicit. The Master himself says: "No man cometh to the Father but by me." And again: "The Father judgeth no man, but hath committed all judgment to the Son, that all men should honour the Son, even as they honour the Father. He that honoureth not the Son honoureth not the Father which hath sent him." And finally, speaking by Paul: "And whatsoever ye do, do it heartily as to the Lord, and not unto men, knowing that of the Lord ye shall receive the reward of the inheritance, for ye serve the Lord Christ," (John xiv. 6; v. 22, 23; Col. iii. 24, 25.)

3. *The Scriptures are a complete and perfect rule of obedience.*—The main design, indeed, of divine revelation is to teach men their condition and state before God, and to lead them back, by the discoveries they make of the glory, majesty, supremacy, holiness, and mercy of God, to Him as the fountain of life, the only source of permanent blessedness. They also reveal the fact that in a future state the common relations and occupations of the present state shall have no place, and yet it is apparent in every part of the sacred volume that it is designed to shed its light upon every one of

these so long as they are to engage the attention of men, and to enforce, even here, exclusive devotion of mind, heart and effort, to the service of God. It is a plausible but very superficial view of the Book of God, and its design, to imagine that it slights the affairs of time, as utterly unworthy of its regard in comparison with things eternal. The truth is, the law—the revealed will and law of God —covers the entire existence of man, and is intended to furnish all the instruction requisite for the right exercise of every faculty, the right use of every gift, in whatever condition and circumstances, man, the creature of God, is placed by the hand of his Maker, and also to enforce its instruction by the paramount authority of Him who is the "only Potentate."

So far then is it from being true that the Christian is to disregard the movements of society, or even what relates to matters of civil regimen, and human rights and liberty, that the very opposite is a truth, and a most important one. The Christian should, of all men, regard things like these with a constant and active interest. So his Bible teaches him—for its pages abound in directions bearing immediately upon them. So soon as he opens its pages, his eye lights upon some truth, law, maxim, warning or example, which he may and should apply to the ordinary interests of time. Hence,

4. *The Bible is the great security of all social order.*—The Bible, of course, read, studied, believed, and made "the man of our counsel." It must be so; for it guards on the one hand, when fairly interpreted, the rights of the individual; it allows of no tyrannical exercise of power, forbidding all oppression, and elevating every human being to his true position of dignity and worth as intelligent and immortal; bringing all down to the same level as guilty before God, and utterly alienated from Him; raising again all the penitent and the believing alike to the highest place of privilege and of hope. Consequently it abases pride, restrains gross and vulgar ambition, teaches mutual esteem, and enjoins mutual interest and good offices.

But on the other hand, the Bible enforces with its sanctions a due arrangement, connexion and subordination in human society. Ever maintaining the prerogatives of an enlightened conscience, it offers no toleration to the vicious, the malevolent, the disorderly, the seditious. It not only restrains them by clear discoveries of the wrath of God, which inevitably attends and visits lawlessness and crime, but, in addition, arms lawful authority with the right to inflict punishment proportioned to the nature and circumstances of offences against social order and moral law. It establishes all just authority; parental, ecclesiastical and civil.

These properties of the Word of God, properly considered, enable us to see why it is that tyrants fear it; that despotic governments oppose its free circulation. It sets up a standard of judgment as the guide of human action infinitely above the enactments of mere human power. It divests man of a superstitious and debasing reverence for arbitrary rule. It exalts, as to the greatest and most desirable issues, the poorest and humblest to a level with the highest. It brings all alike before the same just and impartial tribunal. And, hence, a community imbued with scriptural knowledge can never become the prey of arbitrary power. Such a people will scorn and cast off the yoke of ignoble bondage. But for the same reason, the Bible ever imparts an unshaken stability to free and equitable social and political arrangements, for it teaches men their several duties, discloses to them the beneficent ends of governmental institutions, and endues them with the dispositions and sobriety requisite to, and that go to make, a stable order of society. The free seek and promote, as the best safeguard of liberty, the knowledge of that very Bible which the aristocratic and selfish would put under restraint.

All history confirms these views, and hence the instructive lesson: study, spread, reverence the in-

spired volume, for in it we have this life, as well
as life eternal.

SECTION VII.

OBJECTIONS ANSWERED.

Our interpretation has brought out very distinctly the principle *that no immoral civil power can
demand, at least from any of Paul's teachings in
this passage, the conscientious allegiance and subjection of the citizen.* This principle does not meet
with ready acceptance. Many who admit, and
teach that the obedience due to human authority
is in every case to be limited to things in themselves lawful—that is, not contrary to the law of
God—do still insist that even in the case of an
immoral government—a government, for example,
that sanctions or practises oppression, that refuses
to acknowledge the Most High, his law and his
Son, that sustains false religion, or gives its influence to corrupt forms of Christianity, that winks
at and protects flagrant idolatry, that is administered, mainly, by ungodly men; still even such
a government is to be recognised as God's, and
as such to be obeyed for " conscience' sake." The
advocates of this principle are neither few nor un-
influential. They comprise a very great majority,
not of the godless alone, who view all things ir-

respective of their moral aspects and character, but also of the members and ministers of the Christian churches. Indeed, the opposite opinion, that which we have drawn from the passage, as at least fairly implied in it, is regarded as extreme and fanatical. To this, then, we will direct some attention, and will likewise endeavour, in this connexion, to vindicate the truth of our leading principle in the interpretation of this passage.

It is, surely, rather an ungracious task for any Christian to undertake to defend the principle that God recognises as exemplifications of His ordinance of civil rule, governments of such a character as most of those now existing on earth—to teach that Christ, by his apostle, has enjoined obedience to civil powers, irrespective of their moral character—that whether a government accords with the divine institution of magistracy, or not, it is to be honoured as God's—that the thunderings of divine wrath against those who "resist" authority are directed equally against such as refuse to acknowledge God-forgetting and man-oppressing authorities, and those who endeavour to overthrow or bring into contempt such as are based upon righteousness, and are administered with equity and in the fear of God. Yet such expositors there are.—And

1. *Some assert that the command to be subject is*

unrestricted, and unlimited. Says Haldane, "They (Christians) are bound to obey not good rulers only, as Dr. McKnight unwarrantably limits the word, *but oppressive rulers also.*" " The people of God ought to consider resistance to the government under which they live as a very awful crime, even as a resistance to God himself." * The only limitation he admits—the only excepted case—is when a government commands a sinful act.

It is unnecessary to enter here upon a very minute examination of these singular assertions. The age will not bear them. The voice of suffering humanity is raised against them, and true piety revolts at such a partnership in iniquity and wrong, as such a doctrine charges upon the Most High. However, we remark, (1.) If this were true, then Moses and the Israelites did an immense wrong in setting themselves against Pharaoh and his government. God "raised up" Pharaoh. The Israelites had gone voluntarily into Egypt—and had been long—for some centuries—under the Egyptian government. What then? Did God send Moses to excite a lawless sedition? to heap dishonour upon a government stamped with his own authority? If not, then have we a clear instance of a lawful trampling under foot of unjust power—a

* Commentary on the passage.

righteous refusal to obey a government under which the Israelites had been born and reared. (2.) This writer, and he is not alone, makes no distinction between a government which exists in God's providence merely, and a government which accords with His will, and answers the ends, in due measure, of His institution of magistracy. Let Haldane's principle be universally applied, if applied at all: let no resistance be made to the robber, or to the midnight assassin; for the same providence permits—the same providence is concerned in their assaults and bloodthirsty violence, as in "raising up" a Pharaoh or a Nero. (3.) Such an interpretation runs counter, among others, to the following passage of Scripture: "Shall the throne of iniquity have fellowship with thee, which frameth mischief by a law?" (Ps. xciv. 20.)

2. *Some assert that the only government that may be lawfully resisted is one tyrannical and oppressive;* that is, if a government regard the common rules of equity in its laws and administration, it is to be obeyed for conscience' sake, let its character otherwise be never so godless. On this we remark, (1.) *That* it admits the propriety of applying some test to existing institutions. It abandons the

10

principle of unquestioning subjection to any and every existing institution. For, once admit that character is to be looked after at all, and we not only establish a new rule as our guide, but we absolutely discard, *ipso facto*, the doctrine that a mere providential existence is to be regarded in the matter. If it should, it avails the oppressor as well as the benefactor who occupies the throne and holds the sceptre; for the *same providence*, we repeat, has brought both into being, and invested them with the functions and insignia of power. Moreover, the admission, and we believe it is now generally made, is one of no little practical moment. By the use of this test, we at once set aside as God-given and reverend, such governments as the Austrian, the Russian, the Tuscan, the Neapolitan, the Papal, the Turkish—and, in a word, all the despotic, and Popish powers of the old world and the new. Nor will the government of this land bear well this test. A constitution that throws its shield over the crime of slave-holding, which puts, to nearly all intents and purposes, three millions of its population out of the pale of its protection, surrendering them to a bondage tenfold more bitter than that of Egypt, has need to tremble lest the doom of the oppressor overwhelm it. (2.) The objection overlooks the fact that this passage describes a moral government.

That the passage does so, we have already endeavoured to show. It exhibits a magistrate ruling as God's minister, administering laws which countenance good works and discourage the evil. It is an exceedingly unfair interpretation that would present the apostle as defining civil government as concerned only about breaches of the public peace. The common sense of all enlightened communities repudiates such an exposition. Hence the encouragement given by such to science; the institution and support of schools and colleges, and kindred efforts for the promotion of the public intelligence: and direct efforts also—as in legislation against intemperance and its causes—in behalf of morals. No government among a professedly Christian people has yet been able or, perhaps, disposed, to fall into the limits which *in theory* certain expounders set around it.

But by what right does any one assert that a practical vindication of human rights is sufficient to render a government valid, while it utterly neglects the acknowledgment of God and of his Christ? or if it names Him, does so merely, or mainly, to establish its own claims, while practically regardless of Him? or, perhaps, while professing to honour Christ, gives its sanction and aid to some corrupted form of Christianity, or to anti-Christ himself? or, finally, which puts true religion and false, Christ and Belial, on the same level? Surely that cannot be "the ordinance of God," which gives to God no such honour as he claims—nor that ruler "the minister of God," who distributes his favours alike, in his political regimen, to the faithful disciples of Christ, and the votaries of the "Mother of harlots." And still more plainly, how can that government be God's, which makes no reference to His law, as of paramount authority, but claims for itself absolute supremacy?

We *must* take the character of the government into the account—its character as here described—in making up our judgment upon this matter of subjection, its limits and restrictions. Gross injustice has been done the inspired writer by such authors as Haldane, in neglecting this plain canon of interpretation. And here it may be asked, How can we account for it that the class of expositors with whom we have now to do, *leave out*, or give little weight to the very circumstance which Paul himself adduces as a main proof of the duty of subjection, the equity, industry, and discriminating character of the magistracy, and *introduce* another—the will of the people—which is not referred to here in words, at all? The only account we can give of this most flagrant inconsistency is, that advocacy of free government is now popular, while the law of God, and the supremacy of Christ, are as much hated as ever. In an age when human rights were little heard of, none of this class of interpreters said any thing about such a limitation. In this age, when the language of men and nations is, "We will not have Christ to reign over us," the true *point* of the passage is slurred over, or misinterpreted. We cannot so "handle" the Word of God. It would look too much like that "deceitful handling" of divine revelation which Paul repudiates and condemns, (2 Cor. iv. 2.) That the consent of the people is necessary to render a government legitimate, we strenuously maintain; but this passage makes no reference to this aspect of the question. It deals with the duty of subjection, and by a very clear and comprehensive exhibition of the true nature, functions and *character* of government, both enforces and *limits* the duty.

3. *It is objected that even governments, in the main bad, still do some good, and are better than none, and that, hence, they are to be respected and obeyed.* We have already admitted that absolute perfection is not to be looked for in any government framed and administered by human hands, and that, of course, the want of it is not enough

10*

to invalidate the authority of a magistracy. Nor do we attempt to draw a theoretical line of distinction, so distinct and definite, as to rid the settlement of the question regarding the validity of any particular government of all practical difficulty. It is here as it is in reference to the Church. Her constitution, as it lies in the Word of God, is perfect; but defects still exist in the best churches. And it is far from easy—is it possible?—to prepare a minute statement of the marks of a true church, which will render easy the task of deciding in *every* case, absolutely and *at once*, whether a society can be reckoned a true church or not. And yet every intelligent Christian admits that a church, once genuine in its character, may become completely apostate. To draw the line and say, just *here*, it ought to be abandoned, is not easy. The truth is, all questions of this sort must, as they occur, be left for decision, under the guidance of general principles, such as those to which reference has already been made frequently in these pages, to the enlightened judgment, pure hearts, and honest purposes of the faithful in Christ.

But, to come to the objection, we remark:—(1.) That the objection proves much more than the objector would himself be willing to admit,* for no

* We make no reference here to such expositors as Haldane. He would carry out the objection to the

government ever has, or could exist, that did *no* good to any portion of the community. The most rampant tyranny must have its instruments. These will have their affairs guarded, and their disputes and controversies settled, and, perhaps, fairly. Even a band of pirates cannot dispense altogether with justice. If the doing of some good constitutes a valid claim to allegiance, then is resistance to tyrants, not according to the current maxim, "obedience to God," but, *in every case*, arrant and damnable rebellion. The objection proves too much. Every friend of liberty rejects it. (2.) It takes for granted, which is not true, that the removal of a bad government must be succeeded by anarchy. This is impossible—for any appreciable length of time any how. In every revolution provisional authorities are at once established, and their character will be determined, and their policy controlled, by the character and the object of the revolutionists. They *must* organize, and one of their first aims will always be to remove the causes which gave rise to a desire for a change of the government. Abuses may follow, as did in the French revolution of 1789; but these will find their correction; for so-

farthest extreme. We have in our eye the great mass of the upholders of existing governments, and particularly that portion of those with whom we are in closer contact.

ciety cannot long remain unsettled, nor will it long, when it has the power in its own hands, tolerate gross evil against its own order and quiet. But still more. That class of citizens, who can alone be regarded as wishing to remodel a godless government, must be guided by a regard for God and his rights. If they should withdraw from an active co-operation with existing institutions, it will be mainly for the purpose of introducing Bible elements into the affairs of state. *They* will not tolerate anarchy.

Nor can it be said, that after all, so long as the government exists, its evils are compensated by its good; that it still furnishes such a degree of protection to the citizen as to warrant and require him to own its claims. True, the state of things may be such that the immediate duty of the faithful may be to do no more than withhold allegiance— labouring in the mean time to establish in the minds of all, governors and governed, sound principles on the subject of social and political arrangements. This may even be acknowledged to be the course generally marked out for them by God's word and providence. But, surely, if the community can be rightly taught, and have been taught to understand their duty, and admit it, no reason can be given why the requisite steps should not at once be taken for making the desired change. A new order of things may and ought to arise.

Hoadly was pressed by the same objection in his controversy with the advocates of "passive obedience and non-resistance." He thus replies:— "There would be some colour in this objection, were there no middle condition between tyranny and anarchy, or were it impossible to oppose princes without running into a lawless and ungoverned condition. But I see no necessity of any such thing. And supposing that sometimes a people had, (through the bad designs and evil dispositions of some men,) thrown off tyranny, and run into confusion, or to a tyranny as bad as the former, this is no reason why any people should endure a present tyranny. For this unhappiness doth not necessarily follow, in the nature of the thing, but is purely accidental, and may, with prudence, be prevented— and they must answer for it who are the causes of it. This is just as the church of Rome would affrighten Christians from the most just separations, by telling them that any church tyranny is better than infinite confusion and numberless separations, which are seen to follow without stop, when separation on any account is allowed of. If it be said here, as it may be by some, that any church tyranny is indeed better than separation, which brings confusion with it,—but we are not here left at liberty, for sinful terms are imposed upon us, and we cannot enjoy the means of public worship without complying actually in sin, and therefore there is a necessity of separating, which cannot be said in the case of resistance. If this, I say, be replied, I answer, first, that we see from hence that a practice may be lawful, notwithstanding that the consequence of it may be confusion and anarchy: and then what doth this objection, taken by itself, signify towards the proving my doctrine false? And in the next place our separation, or reformation, with all its consequences, is better than a passive submission to the exorbitant power and tyranny of the Church of Rome, even supposing no terms of external communion absolutely sinful imposed upon us. For as it is exercised in manifold, notorious and scandalous instances, who can prove submission to it to be so much as lawful? And therefore, thirdly, who can prove it so much as lawful to pay such a submission to any mortal upon earth, as helps to ruin and destroy the rights of others, which we cannot honourably give up, though we may our own, the rights and happiness of our neighbours, of all our countrymen, and of all posterity to come? This must be done by other arguments. But the making this objection is only just, as if one should say to a man dying of a fever, you may indeed be cured of this disease by some particular remedies, but you had better let it take its course, for sometimes it hath been seen that when they have removed that distemper they have thrown the patient into another as bad, or worse, by pure accident, and through want of due care and prudence. In fine, it doth not in the least follow that because the guarding against one evil hath sometimes accidentally, and without any necessity, brought on another, therefore we may not, in prudence, defend ourselves against it, when we may likewise, if we be not wanting to ourselves, keep off the other also. But were the doctrine I have taught universally and publicly embraced, I am persuaded the ground of all such objections would be removed, because the whole foundation of tyranny would be destroyed, unless where there is supposed a force sufficient to bear it out."*

(3.) If this objection be true, no revolution could ever occur, for surely, before any can attempt a radical change of government, and this is the case supposed—they must have previously become convinced that the existing authorities have no claim upon their conscientious support. Take, as an example, the English Revolution of 1688. Before

* Hoadly, pp. 75, 76, 77.

adopting measures for the expulsion of James II., the leaders in that transaction must first have seen it to be their duty to refuse him their allegiance. Had they still regarded him as God's "minister," they could not have laid their plans—with a good conscience—to remove him from the throne. And, yet, even then, who can question that James' government yielded much good to the British nation, in the way of preserving the peace, and in guarding the private interests of the people of England. And, now, we add, had this revolution failed, would its abettors have become bound to return, *in heart*, to their allegiance? All the reasons would still have existed by which they had been fully satisfied that a revolution was necessary. Would they have been bound to discard their previous judgment? Certainly not. Success or failure in a righteous attempt—and all sound Protestants, except a few Haldanes, admit this to have been a righteous one—does not decide a question of morals or of religion.

The illustration is precisely in point. Other governments may not be liable to just the same objections as was the British administration; but to others equally valid. Their oppression may be different in form—their relations to religion, and treatment of the church different, and, moreover, the mass of the people may go along with them in these things. But what then? The question is, Do they oppress knowingly and obstinately? Do they slight and dishonour religion? Do they bestow their favours upon any kind of false religion? Do they disregard God and repudiate the paramount authority of His Bible? Are they guilty of any or of all of these sins? If so, then, whether they be few or many, the friends of liberty, of religion, and of God, should withhold from them their conscientious obedience; for they are not "a terror to evil doers, and a praise to them that do well." This cannot be denied, we repeat, except upon grounds that would entirely destroy the right of civil revolution.

4. *It is affirmed that the tenor of scriptural example, and some of the teachings of Christ, are against our doctrine.* (1.) The principal examples are those of Joseph and Daniel in accepting and exercising authority in heathen kingdoms. On these we remark, that in their cases there is every reason to believe that there was no obligation incurred by either of them to conform to any immoral law, and that in their administration, the law of God was in fact made, so far as their own particular functions were concerned, the rule of their administration. They had nothing to do with any

11

thing but the duties of their own office. Neither directly or indirectly were they required to concur in the idolatries of those nations or to sanction any acts of oppression. These and similar cases are thus disposed of by a late writer.*

"Any office may be held, or service engaged in, upon the three following conditions:

"1st. That the duties belonging to it be right in themselves.

"2d. That they be regulated by a just law.

"3d. That there be no other oath of office required, but faithfully to execute official duties. Let these be the stipulations, and an office may be held under any power, however immorally constituted, without a homologation of its immorality.

"Suppose I were in Algiers, residing there at pleasure; would my accepting an office from the Dey, under the regulations now specified, say a professorship in a university instituted by him, for the instruction of youth, be a homologation of his immoral regency—naval piracy—or the blood and murder upon which his throne is erected? If there as a *slave*, would not the appointment be still more eligible? This corresponds with the situation of the captives in Babylon: it does not,

* From "Sons of Oil," by Sam. B. Wylie, late of Philadelphia.

therefore, follow, that holding an office necessarily supposes, either that the government be lawful, or if not, that the person holding the office is implicated in the immorality."

"If it be pleaded that the monarch's will was the constitution, this, even if admitted, makes no difference. The office was either such as required allegiance to this constitution, or it did not. If the latter, it is the thing contended for, viz., that there was no immoral obligation connected with his office. If the former, he was perjured, not only by breaking it in several instances, but in taking it also, for he swore to a blank, i. e., to perform he knew not what. But there is no account of Daniel's coming under any such obligation. Indeed, it would have been inconsistent with the smiles of Heaven, which he, and others in office, evidently enjoyed."

(2.) Reference is made to the language and conduct of Christ, Matt. xvii. 24—27; and Matt. xxii. 21. In the former we have an account of the paying of a certain tribute, and in the latter we have the reply of Christ to an inquiry put by the Pharisees, when he says, "Render to Cæsar the things that are Cæsar's." To these we reply in the words of the writer just quoted.

"The allegation brought from Matt. xvii. 27, is

evidently unfounded. The best commentators consider the tribute here mentioned to be temple money, the ransom of the soul spoken of, Exod. xxx. 12, 13. That this was the case will appear evident, first, because the piece of money found in the fish's mouth is allowed, by the best critics, to be equal in value to two half shekels, one for Christ, and the other for Peter. And, secondly, from the argument by which our Lord pleads exemption, namely, from the example of the kings of the earth. 'What thinkest thou, Simon? Of whom do the kings of the earth take custom or tribute? Of their own children, or of strangers? Peter saith unto him, Of strangers. Jesus saith unto him, Then are the children free.' Here we find, by the example of earthly kings, Christ was free. How was he free? By being the Son to the King to whom the tribute belonged. Who was this King? It could not be Cæsar. Was Christ Cæsar's son? No. For had he been Cæsar's son, it must have been either by natural generation, adoption or citizenship. None of all these was the case. And even though the last had taken place, which is the only plausible supposition, (though false,) it would not have procured this immunity, because citizenship did not exempt from tribute. But Jesus was the Son of the God of heaven, that King to whom this tribute belonged; hence he says, 'notwithstanding,' that is, though I am free, by the relation of Sonship," &c.

"The other allegation brought from Matt. xxii. 21, 'Render to Cæsar the things that are Cæsar's,' &c., is equally unfounded. It is abundantly evident, from the passage, that the question was intended to ensnare the Lord Jesus Christ, answer as he would. It was proposed by the Herodians and Pharisees; those, votaries for Roman domination, and these, the sticklers for Jewish immunities. Had he said, 'Give it to Cæsar,' the Pharisees, ever ready to accuse him, would have represented him to the people as an enemy to their ancient privileges. Had he said, 'Don't give it,' the Herodians would have represented him to Herod as an enemy to the government of Cæsar. In the fifteenth verse, we are expressly told they came to him with a view to 'entangle him in his talk.' But he, 'knowing their craftiness,' split their dilemma, and left their question unde-, cided. He, on several other occasions, thus baffled his adversaries; as in John viii. 4, 12, in the case of the 'woman taken in adultery;' and in Luke xii. 14, when application was made to him concerning the settlement of the earthly inheri-

11*

tance. It is objected here, by some, 'that this explanation of our Saviour's answer represents the Lord as shunning to declare the whole counsel of God—giving no answer in a case respecting sin and duty.' The inference is false. They were not without information on this very subject. They had the law and the prophets. The Lord Jesus Christ had given specific directions concerning the character of lawful rulers, Deut. xvii. 15, to whom it was lawful to pay tribute for conscience' sake. But it was not information they wanted, but to ensnare him, let him answer as he would, as has already been shown. If silence, or refusing to answer in every case, even in matters respecting sin and duty, let the design of the querist be what it will, be accounted criminal, in what point of light will the objector view the Lord Jesus Christ, when he finds him actually refusing to answer a question respecting sin and duty, in the case of his own authority? Mark xi. 27, 33. 'Neither do I tell you (says he) by what authority I do these things.' It would be well if men would consider the awful consequences of some of their objections before they make them. But, supposing that Christ, in both the instances alluded to, had commanded tribute to be paid to Cæsar, what does it prove? Unless he commanded it to be paid as a *tessera* of loyalty, it proves no more the morality of Cæsar's right, than a minister of the gospel's advising one of his hearers to give the robber part of his property, to secure the remainder, would, that the minister considered the robber morally entitled to it."*

Hoadly says, "But it is manifest that it was not his design to tell his adversaries, (whose ensnaring question was the occasion of this precept,) what his opinion was concerning the rights of the emperor, but only to evade the danger of such an answer as they hoped to have extorted from him."†

(3.) Paul's appeal to Cæsar has also been adduced as importing an acknowledgment of his right to rule. On this we use again the words of the Sons of Oil.

"To this I answer, an appeal to their tribunals no more involves in it a homologation of their lawful dominion, than an appeal from a murderer to a thief, who would be disposed to save one's life, would be a homologation of his living habitually in the breach of the eighth commandment. Suppose, for example, that the Allegheny mountains were infested with a banditti of robbers, whose captain retained still so much humanity as to esta-

* Sons of Oil, pp. 82—84.   † Hoadly, p. 120.

blish a law that no poor man should be robbed of more than ten dollars—you happen to be crossing the mountain—five of the gang approach you, and rob you of one hundred, which is nearly your all— you meet with the master of the fraternity—you know the law—and believe that he still has as much humanity remaining as will induce him to execute it.   Will you appeal to him to cause your ninety dollars to be refunded, which are due to you by his own law?   If you do, will this implicate you in the immorality of the banditti, or be saying Amen to their unlawful practice?   Certainly not.   If this hold in the greater, it will surely hold in the less.   If an appeal may be made to the captain of a band of robbers, without implication in his criminality, much more to these institutions, which, though wrong in some fundamentals, are yet aiming at the good of civil society."*

5. *It is confidently asserted that the Roman Christians must have understood the Apostle as referring to the Roman government—enjoining subjection to it.*   This is, perhaps, the prime objection, after all, to the views we have presented of the scope and bearing of this passage, and deserves a tolerably minute examination.   And, (1.)

* Sons of Oil, pp. 81, 82.

The description here given of the magistrate does not correspond to that of the reigning Emperor of Rome, nor to the character of his administration. Nor are any so ignorant as to be without some knowledge of the character and doings of Nero Cæsar—that he was a human monster; a bloody persecutor; a tyrant so remorseless that even pagan Rome ultimately dethroned and put him to death. How could it be said by Paul, speaking of such a man, "That he was a terror, not to good works, but to the evil?"—"a minister of God to thee for good?" We again quote Hoadly: "If any should say that he speaks particularly of the Roman Emperor who, at this time, was a very bad man, I answer, if he were such a magistrate as did set himself to destroy the happiness of the people under him, and to act contrary to the end of his office, it is impossible that Paul should mean him particularly in this place. For the higher powers, v. 1, are the same with the rulers, v. 3, and whomsoever Paul intended, he declares to be, not a terror to good works, but to the evil. So that if the Roman Emperor were a terror to good works, and not to the evil, either Paul was grossly mistaken in his opinion of him, or he could not be particularly meant here. If Paul intended to press obedience to him, particularly, he manifestly doth it upon the supposition, that he was not a terror to good works, but to evil. And if this supposition be destroyed, the reasoning built upon it must fall, and all the obligation to subjection that is deduced from it."*

(2.) The scriptures clearly describe the Roman government as despotic, ungodly and bestial. "After this I saw, in the night visions, and, behold, a fourth beast, dreadful and terrible, and strong exceedingly; and it had great iron teeth; it devoured and brake in pieces, and stamped the residue with the feet of it; and it was diverse from all beasts that were before it; and it had ten horns." (Dan. vii. 7.) "And I stood upon the sand of the sea, and saw a beast rise up out of the sea, having seven heads and ten horns; and upon his horns ten crowns; and upon his heads the name of blasphemy." (Rev. xiii. 1.) All sound Protestant expositors unite in applying these prophecies to the Roman Empire. That they should be so applied ought not to be questioned. Now, is it possible that the same Spirit who dictated these prophecies, did also teach Paul to delineate this savage beast of prey, "dreadful and terrible," as a "terror to evil doers, and a praise to them that do well?" The thing is incredible. "Doth a

* Hoadly, p. 48.

fountain send forth, at the same hole, sweet water and bitter?" is the inquiry of an inspired writer. Does the blessed Spirit send forth teachings so diametrically opposite? We cannot believe it. He gives the true character of this huge and destroying power in the book of Daniel, as it rages among the nations—trampling and rending them, and gorging itself with their blood. Such a power He never claims as His. The passage before us cannot apply to Rome.*

(3.) It cannot, because one part of the mission of the gospel was and is to overthrow and utterly demolish it. For this purpose, among others, Christ reigns. This, also, was long before revealed. "And in the days of these kings shall the God of heaven set up a kingdom which shall never be destroyed; and the kingdom shall not be left to other people, but it shall break in pieces and consume all these kingdoms." (Dan. ii. 44.) "These,"—the ten horns—"shall make war with the Lamb, and he shall overcome them." (Rev. xvii. 14.) But why quote? Throughout the whole prophetic scriptures—both Old Testament and New—this great, ungodly, tyrannical, persecuting and blasphemous power, is presented as the object of divine wrath, to be consumed, together

* See Appendix D.

with the "little horn," (Dan. viii.)—or the "two-horned beast," (Rev. xiii.)—by the word and by the judgment of God—to be consumed for its iniquities committed against God and his gospel. Did the Spirit of Christ enjoin upon Christians a conscientious "fear," "honour," and obedience, to a system against which the Bible teems with the weightiest denunciations?

These inquiries assume a deeper meaning and importance, if we remember that the passage before us enjoins not mere "submission," but a true support and co-operation—that it is not left optional to withhold these from the "powers" designated in the text. Now, is it credible that Paul intended to teach that Christians should incorporate with the Roman Empire? Even the "body of the beast" is to be "given to the burning flame." (Dan. vii. 11.) And, again, in Rev. (chap. xiii. 8,) it is said that "all that dwell on the earth shall worship him (the seven-headed and ten-horned beast) whose names *are not written in the book of life.*" We cannot conceive that the same God who moved John thus to write, did, but a generation before, inspire Paul to command Christians to incorporate with this same beast and become constituents of his empire.

(4.) We are not without very express testimony

that the primitive Christians were not countenanced in doing—were even forbidden to do certain acts which might be regarded as importing an acknowledgment of the claims of Rome. "Dare any of you," says Paul, (1 Cor. vi. 1,) "having a matter against another, go to law before the unjust and not before the saints?" It cannot be disputed that the settlement of pecuniary matters and disputes, is one of the functions of civil government. This was contemplated in its institution. And we cannot imagine how it could be wrong in the Christian to appeal for redress to any ordinance of God in reference to such matters as lie within its own province. God set up a civil government in Israel. Before its courts, Jews were to implead one another. To the civil tribunals they were to bring, as their proper place, all civil causes. When civil government is purified—and it yet will be—all such controversies will be settled by its action. Why then does Paul forbid the Corinthians making such a reference of their personal affairs to the Roman tribunals? Can it be accounted for on any other principle than this? that such proceedings would, at least, appear to involve them in an acknowledgment of their right to administer law to Christians, as being to them the ordinance of God. Moreover, he calls

12

the Roman magistrates "the unjust." Did he, then, at one time, so speak of them, and, shortly after, urge upon Christians a conscientious subjection to their authority and maintenance of their government, inasmuch as they were a "terror to evil doers, and a praise to them that do well?" Assuredly not. In a word, Paul enjoins upon the Corinthians to withhold from the tribunals of the Roman empire a part of that "honour" which certainly belongs to all recognised governments; and, in so doing, establishes a principle that would operate, with no little power, in keeping them and the Christians separate from the community in which they lived— that would remind them that while *in*, they were not *of*, the Roman State.

Now, much of all this that we have adduced in the last few pages, was before the minds of the Romans. They knew that Daniel had described that government as bestial—they had heard, no doubt, of the directions given to the Christians of Corinth—they understood, and to this we particularly refer, that the Roman Emperor and government were idolatrous and oppressive—that the gospel was preached, often at the hazard of life, and that its profession even was extensively discountenanced. How would they, then, understand this chapter? We put, in reply, another interrogatory. How would the inhabitants of Papal Rome—the city itself—now understand the very same teachings? We address them: "Brethren—be subject to the higher powers. They are the ministers of God to thee for good. They are a terror to evil doers, and a praise to them that do well. Do that which is good, and thou shalt have praise of the same." What would they say? We can easily imagine their countenances, at first marked with some astonishment. "Can this be our government? No! it cannot. Are not our friends—the friends of the Bible—banished or executed? Are we not deprived of our liberties? Have we not seen deeds—do we not witness them almost daily—of the grossest oppression? Are not evil doers in high places? Are not the God-fearing regarded with jealousy? Is not the Bible—God's own book—a forbidden volume? Is not the gospel hated and opposed, and idolatry publicly practised and protected? No. It cannot be that Pius IX. and his ghostly government are here described, and that we are commanded, on pain of damnation, to support, fear and honour them."

To what conclusions would intelligent minds come? Why, certainly, to this, that, whatever the import of the passage, it could not apply to their governors. So would a godly Austrian—so a Hungarian—so a Spaniard—so a *slave* in the United States. Hence we add—

(5.) To apply this to the Roman government is to dishonour religion. It is time that religion—the true religion—was rid of this reproach. It is doing no little evil. Convince men that any government that happens to exist, whatever its character, is to be obeyed, honoured and reverenced; we mean that the Bible enjoins this, and you have struck a very heavy blow at the Bible itself. Men—if they believe in God at all—cannot believe He is the patron of iniquity and wrong. And, hence, they will refuse to recognise the claims of any book that professes to come from God, and yet so represents him.

But of what use, then, was this passage? Why did it find a place in this epistle? Why in the volume of inspiration at all? We answer: [1.] That it was designed to show that civil government is not, as an institution, abolished by the advent of the Messiah and the setting up of his kingdom among Gentile nations. In other words, that the ecclesiastical was not the only social power—that civil society was not to be absorbed by the church. It was important to state this distinctly;

for there has ever been a tendency developed, in connexion with every great religious movement, to depreciate the *institution* of magistracy—to regard it as beneath the Christian to pay any respect to political regimen, or, in any circumstances, to take a part in managing civil affairs, except so far as they may be connected with the government of the church. This spirit was, unquestionably, developed in the church at a very early period. It made its appearance during the Reformation in Germany, in Holland, and in England. It is sometimes seen among the quite intelligent now, who suppress, in their own minds, all interest in political movements, not so much from conviction respecting their practical or doctrinal corruptions, as from a mistaken notion that they are not spiritual enough at least for the devout and godly.

Every disposition of this sort is rebuked by this passage. It stands with a few parallel passages; and has stood ever, as an impregnable bulwark against such delusive notions.

[2.] It furnished then, as now, a standard by which to try existing governments. That it was not intended to induce them to "honour"—and reverence and sustain, the imperial authority of Nero, we have already endeavoured to show. They could not so understand it. At first, they might

12*

be somewhat surprised—but soon—upon a little reflection, they would see that in these verses the Apostle had really furnished a very clear mirror in which they could see, by contrast, the hideous features of the "beastly" power of Rome. It is of use in this way still. The lineal descendants of the ancient Italians, who cannot discern in their own rulers, as we have seen, any traces of the beneficent power here described, may learn most important lessons. They may find that governments, whatever claim of divine right they set up, are not above the examination of the Christian citizen—and, more than this, here are the very tests to apply.

[3.] It presented then, and does now, the specific ends which the godly should seek to attain in their reforming efforts. It has been already hinted that the word of God, the gospel of Christ, is intended to overthrow immoral and despotic power. It will do more : it will accomplish a complete reformation; and this by the instrumentality of well instructed and faithful men, who labour with an intelligent eye to a fixed and definite end. This end they find here. Not only here, for it appears elsewhere in the inspired record; but here stated with singular definiteness, distinctness and brevity. Setting this before them, the friends of Christ and of the welfare of man are engaged in no aimless work. Their toils in this department of their efforts have this as their object—the ultimate establishment of governmental authority that shall honour God and religion, shall enact just laws, protecting the poor, and restraining all wrong, and that shall seek as their highest aim to advance the name and glory of Christ.

[4.] The Christians in Rome would find here ample reason for the study of quietness and patience and the sedulous discharge of all the common duties of life; for here is seen, with the utmost clearness, the importance of civil society, and the imperative character of social duties. Here the fact is presented in the boldest relief, that the commission of crime, the unnecessary disturbance of the peace of the community, such conduct as denominates one a "bad citizen," whether in the narrower or the wider sense of the phrase, is deserving of "wrath;" that the practice of the Christian virtues—what these are we learn elsewhere—meets with commendation: is pleasing to God.

Hence, it may be added, the wise student of Rom. xiii. 1—7, will rise from his investigations deeply impressed on the one hand with the wide departures from its high standard which have characterized and do yet characterize, the kingdoms of this world, and, of course, with a confirmed determination to refuse them his active support, but, on the other hand, with a profound and salutary conviction of the excellence of the *institution* of government, and the weighty responsibilities that rest upon the Christian as he sustains many relations to society around him. He will thus be guarded against a spirit of sedition or lawlessness, and imbued with a disposition to attend to the requirements of duty in his own particular sphere, so that while he may exemplify the faithfulness of the witness for Christ, he may still "lead a quiet and peaceable life in all godliness and honesty." (1 Tim. ii. 2.)

[5.] There is not wanting evidence that the primitive Christians did gather at least much of this sort of instruction from these teachings of Paul. We once more quote Hoadly: "It is very remarkable that Origen, (the same person who challenges Celsus, that great enemy to Christians, to name any sedition, or tumult in which the Christians were concerned,) is by some alleged for this in defence of passive obedience; that he, (I say,) should mention that celebrated passage of Paul, (Rom. xiii. 1,) upon which some have built so much, with such a remark as would incline one to think that all the primitive Christians did not see any such unlimited non-resistance in it as many have done since. The passage I mean is towards the end of his eighth book against Celsus, where he takes occasion to cite this place of Paul, to show the adversaries of Christianity what notions Christians had concerning princes, and the subjection due to them. But he immediately adds that there were many questions and disquisitions about the meaning of this place of Scripture, arising from the consideration of the cruelty and tyranny of many princes; and that upon that account he would not at present undertake to give an exact account of it. From whence I think it manifest, not only that many of the first Christians doubted whether the subjection preached by Paul was due, in point of conscience, to tyrants and oppressors; but also that Origen himself, when he wrote this, did not believe it to be so. For if he did, he had now the fairest occasion for declaring it; and he could not more effectually have defended the Christians from the objections now before him, than by saying so."*

This passage was far from useless to the Romans, though it did not teach them conscientious obedience to a rampant savage power. It taught them

* Hoadly, p. 139.

better things, more becoming Christians. To us it brings the same lessons.

6. It may be objected that to withhold allegiance from ungodly governments is not practicable —that lands must be held—taxes paid—the laws appealed to for redress. We reply, (1.) That property is not held of the state. The state—the nation—does not give the title. Or if it be in any case original proprietor, the purchase of land from the state no more implies a recognition of its other claims than the purchase of property from an individual recognises all his acts, and endorses his character. (2.) Taxes may be paid, either on business principles merely, for work done, or for the reason that if they be not paid, they will be *taken*. Circumstances may occur making it an imperative duty to refuse the payment of taxes at all hazards, but ordinarily this would be unwise because ineffectual, and would answer no end that cannot, at least as well, be otherwise obtained. (3.) The courts may be appealed to on principles already stated and vindicated.* (4.) We reply, in general, to every objection of this sort, that we must distinguish between things that belong merely to matters of social neighbourhood and arrangement, and things governmental; that there is a vast difference be-

* See p. 131.

tween men's availing themselves merely of natural rights, and taking an active and, of course, voluntary part in affairs of state. And, finally, that all these acts, which are comprehended in this class of objections, are acts which aliens may do, and privileges used such as aliens enjoy, and yet no one imagines that the alien becomes, by such acts as buying lands, &c., a corporate member of the body politic.

Our principle will stand the most rigid investigation—it demands the closest examination. For it is a matter of no small moment to ascertain well that we do not so identify ourselves with institutions which dishonour God and oppress man, as to involve ourselves in their guilt and punishment, or weaken our own hands in the efforts we may be disposed to make for their reformation.

CONCLUSION.

And 1. *There is no such sacredness about civil governments as to exempt them from the closest scrutiny in their constitution and workings.* The time was when it would have been necessary to dwell largely upon this statement. The occupants of power are always disposed to claim an uninquiring recognition, as well as an unresisting obedience. Kings and emperors have been addressed by 'the title of "sacred majesty." They have claimed a "divine right" to reign. They are kings "by the grace of God." They are to rule and the people to submit, pay taxes, and bear all the burdens. This was once the theory. Some changes have, indeed, passed over society in many Christian countries. Men do not now yield so readily a blind and superstitious obedience. But, after all, the principle is not yet fully recognised that, like every thing else in human hands, the affairs of government are, in every aspect, open to be questioned and tried. Even in this land, with all its licentiousness of opinion and even contempt of authority, there is yet not a little of the old leaven. Not a few still appear to regard the constitution, and even some enactments, and these the worst of them, as possessing a sort of extraordinary sacredness.

For all this there is no reason. The Church is, surely, as sacred as the state, and yet what friend of religious liberty denies the right of the Lord's freeman to bring her claims to the proof—to try her proceedings? It is one of the hateful peculiarities of the great Apostacy, to demand an uninquiring subjugation of the understanding and conscience to its arrogant demand of implicit recognition and obedience. The faithful repudiate the claim. They have ever insisted that to admit it would be treason against Christ.

Nor in divesting government of *this kind* of sacredness do we furnish any opening for either licentiousness or sedition. The standard—the chief standard—of judgment here, as in all other matters where morals are concerned, is the Word of God. We do not reject reason altogether. But reason itself must be proved by the same word. And it has been previously observed that when the Holy Scriptures are conscientiously regarded and justly applied, the result will be, on the one hand, the rejection of what God does not approve, and on the other hand, the intelligent and hearty subjection of the whole man to what accords with the divine will. And can it be considered as any thing short of an infidel contempt of the Bible to assert that to use it for this purpose is either wrong or dangerous to the peace and order of society?

II. *Tried by this supreme rule, the government of this land cannot claim conscientious obedience.* It has, indeed, been set up by the action, and, of course, exists by the voice of the majority of the people. But this is not the only test. The people may be wrong now, as well as of old, when the ten tribes "set up kings, but not by" God, "and princes,

13

and he knew (approved) it not," (Hosea vii. 3, 4.) That this has been done in these states is evident because the paramount authority of the Most High, speaking in his word, is not recognised in the constitution—the fundamental law of the general government; because Christ is not, in any sense, acknowledged in his character as "Prince of the kings of the earth," (Rev. i. 3;) because the Bible is not received as law, obligatory and supreme; because no barrier has been enacted against the induction of God's enemies into places of power—of trust; because the same securities are thrown around the idolatries of Popery, as around the practice and observances of the true religion; because oppression is sanctioned, and the oppressor protected in the enjoyment of his despotic and unfounded claim.— In this last we refer, of course, to slavery, which is numbered among the "institutions" of nearly one-half of the states, and the constitution gives the same protection to this institution as to any others. It does more. It provides specific and peculiar means for the arrest of the fugitive; or, perhaps, more accurately, it contains provisions, which may be made, and have been, the basis of distinct legislation on this subject.*

* Appendix E.

Now, let it be remembered, that to constitute an oppressive and tyrannical government, it is not requisite that the subjects of the violence and wrong be white men: it is enough if they be men—nor that they be the majority, kept under by a well situated and armed minority, as in Italy or Austria. Any institutions are chargeable with the sin and *crime* of despotism, that wilfully deprive any class of their citizens of their natural rights, or sanction it when done. This is the case here. The constitution treats as outcasts from its pale a large proportion of the inhabitants of the country, more than three millions out of twenty-four. Hence, it is not only wrong and sinful to swear to maintain the constitution: we go farther, and affirm that such a government is not to be "honoured" as God's moral ordinance; it is not,—as it respects a host within its limits, and these belonging to that very class, the poor and needy, for whose protection civil government was eminently designed—a "minister of God for good," but a minister o *evil*. To such a government the apostle has here no reference in his injunctions of obedience. It does not possess the features here required. It possesses some that are here, by implication, strongly condemned.

We are aware that it is no easy task to persuade

men—even intelligent men—that this is a matter in which they have a deep, personal, and responsible interest. The evil of corrupt government is one so nearly universal and of so long standing— the notion is so prevalent that if there is any thing wrong, it is not *their* concern; and the obstacles are often so many and so great in the way of a complete withdrawing from an active share in affairs of state; and, finally, it is so easy to lull the conscience by the delusive idea that the best way to reform a government is first to swear to support it, and to take a part in its operations. In view of all these considerations, it is a matter of labour and of effort, and cannot be accomplished unless the Spirit of God imparts clear and spiritual vision, and gives a decided and resolute will.*

III. *Such as do take this step are called to a position of peculiar difficulty.*—On the one hand they are to watch against doing any thing really inconsistent with the place which they have deliberately occupied—apart from the governmental machinery; at the same time testifying with candour and faithfulness against existing wrong —and yet, on the other hand, they need to be equally watchful lest they be tempted to despise

* See Appendix C.

even the *institution* of government, become regardless of the welfare of the land, or in any way disorderly in their deportment. It is especially required of them that "they follow every good work," and thus by a pure and peaceable behaviour as individuals, and by the exemplariness of their deportment in social life, commend to all men the excellence of a *full* and *faithful* profession of the name of Christ, or at least, that "by well doing, they may put to silence the ignorance of foolish men."

IV. *The doctrines of this passage and the collateral principles to which we have referred, will certainly yet prevail on earth.*—The very fact that Paul was inspired of God to give such a view of civil authority is a guarantee that it shall yet receive a just exemplification. However this may be, other scriptures are more explicit. "The kingdom and dominion, and the greatness of the kingdom under the whole heaven, shall be given to the saints of the Most High." (Dan. vii. 27.) "The kings of Tarshish and of the isles shall bring presents: the kings of Sheba and Seba shall offer gifts. Yea, all kings shall fall down before him; all nations shall serve him. For he shall deliver the needy when he crieth; the poor also, and him that hath no helper. He shall spare the poor and

13*

needy, and shall save the souls of the needy.   He shall redeem their souls from deceit and violence: and precious shall their blood be in his sight." (Ps. lxxii. 10—14.)   "And kings shall be thy nursing fathers, and their queens thy nursing mothers." (Is. xlix. 23.)   "Blessed and holy is he that hath part in the first resurrection: on such the second death hath no power, but they shall be priests of God and of Christ, and shall reign with him a thousand years." (Rev. xx. 6.)   The apostle John thus describes the ultimate issue of the vast changes in reference to things religious, political, and social, in the following most expressive and emphatic language: "The kingdoms of this world are become the kingdoms of our Lord and of his Christ, and he shall reign for ever and ever." (Rev. xi. 15.) Even so come, Lord Jesus.

APPENDIX.

A.—Page 17.

The word "εξουσια" has been a good deal insisted upon as denoting a power lawful before God. It is derived from the verb "εξεστι"—"it is lawful." Still, we would not insist upon this so far as to lay any great stress upon it in argument. It is not necessary to do so; and, moreover, the term is used in Rev. xiii. 3, to express the "authority" of the beast of the sea.

B.—Page 18.

On the word "υπερεχουσαις" more stress may be, perhaps, laid. The following is from a lecture on the Revelation, by *Murray, of Newcastle*, England:—

"There is a passage, which has been much improved by those that imagine that believers of the

13†

Gospel are, by the Apostle, enjoined to yield a passive obedience, and that is in Romans xiii. 1, which version reads, 'Let every soul be subject to the higher powers,' &c., to the beginning of the seventh verse. With all due respect to our translators, and other learned men, I will affirm that this is rather a paraphrase of the translators, than a translation of the text. From the very genius of the Greek language, it is manifest that εξουσιαις υπερεχουσαις do not signify all sorts of authority, but only such as protect men in the enjoyment of their just rights and privileges; and these words ought to be read literally, *protecting authorities*, or *excellent authorities*. Εξουσια, in its first signification, signifies *just and lawful power or authority*, and can never be applied to tyrants and oppressors without abuse: υπερεχω signifies to protect, or to be eminent, and is here understood in that sense, as in other Greek authors. Homer makes use of *this* word in *this sense*, when he describes Agamemnon addressing the Greeks, when the Trojans were advancing against them, (Iliad. iv. l. 249.)—'Will ye tarry,' says he, 'till the Trojans advance, to know whether Jupiter will protect you?' Οφρα ιδητ αικ υμιν υπερσχη χειρα Κρονιων. This Apostle makes use of this word, (Phil. iv. 7,) to point out the excellency of the peace of God. Και ειρηνη του Θεου η υπερεχουσα παντα νουν; *and the peace of 'God which, passeth all understanding, shall keep your hearts.'* This same Apostle, in the second chapter of this Epistle, makes use of the same word to signify excellency, or what is more excellent, or better; αλληλους ηγουμινοι υπιριχοντας, 'let each esteem others better than themselves.' It does not appear from this passage that there is any command to be subject to any powers, except such as excel, and protect their subjects."

C.—Page 46.

Murray takes the same view that we have done of this passage. He says:—

"But let us read the whole paragraph, without any paraphrase in the translation, and see how it will prove non-resistance. 'Let every soul be subordinate to the authorities protecting them; for it is not authority, if not from God. But these that are authorities under God, are appointed. Therefore, he that resisteth the authority resisteth the appointment of God, and they that resist shall receive judgment to themselves. For rulers are not a terror of good works, but of evil. Will you not fear authority? do good, and you shall have praise from it; for he is the servant of God for good. But if you do evil, fear, for he beareth not the sword in vain; for he is the servant of God, a revenger for wrath to him that doeth evil. Therefore, it is necessary to obey, not only for *wrath*, but for *conscience'* sake. For this cause pay you tribute also, for they are the servants of God, waiting continually for this very thing. Render therefore to all their due; tribute to whom tribute, custom to whom custom, fear to whom fear, honour to whom honour.' Can any words make the subject more plain, that it is the appointment of God, and the ruler answering the character here given him, that lays the obligation upon Christians to obey him? If the people who bring Romans xiii. 1, as a proof of mere passive obedience to all sorts of superiors, will please to read the text carefully, the arguments they use will vanish, whether they will or not. It is plain to a demonstration that as the Apostle does not here appoint any particular form of government, so he says nothing of the present rulers, but recommends subjection to governors in general; and that from the consideration of the Divine institution of their office, and the advantage thereof to mankind, when right administered. To resist such governors as answer the end of their office, and the Apostle's representation is, no doubt, a great crime, and deserves a proportionable punishment, called here *κριμα* (*judgment*,) both in this life, and that which is to come. But the resisting of tyranny and tyrants falls not under the sentence of the Apostle. The text says nothing to the case of tyrants, but really excludes them as being another sort of creatures from what he describes, and the very reverse of that character which he gives the minister of God, to whom he requires subjection."

"They are not at all authorities of God, according to the Apostle, if they are a terror to good works, and a praise to evil; for the authorities appointed by God are appointed for this end. And the authority that does not answer this end is not an authority that it is lawful to obey. In such a case, the threatening should be read backwards, namely, 'he that resisteth not the power shall receive (κριμα) *judgment.*' If any person were to read a Greek classic as these advocates for passive obedience read the New Testament, they would be posted up as enemies to true literature and common sense, by all the literati in the three kingdoms. The Apostles have nowhere affirmed, that Christians, at the pleasure of despots, were to surrender their liberties more than others, who were fellow-citizens with them, in the same country. If both the rulers and the rest of the subjects differ with them, they have no other shift but to remonstrate against their oppression, suffer, or forsake their country."

Milton says:—

"The words immediately after make it as clear as the sun, that the Apostle speaks only of a lawful power; for he gives us in them a definition of magistrates, and thereby explains to us who are the persons thus authorized, and upon what account we are to yield obedience, lest we should be apt to mistake, and ground extravagant notions upon his discourse. '*Magistrates,*' says he, '*are not a terror to good works, but to evil. Wilt thou, then, not be afraid of the power? Do that which is good, and thou shalt have praise of the, same; for he is the minister of God to thee for good: he beareth not the sword in vain; for he is the minister of God, a revenger, to execute wrath upon him that doeth evil.'* What honest man would not willingly submit to such a magistracy as is here described, and that not only to avoid wrath, and for fear of punishment, but *for conscience' sake?* Whatever power enables a man, or whatsoever magistrate takes upon him to act contrary to what Paul makes the duty of those that are in authority, neither is that power nor that magistrate ordained of God; and, consequently, to such a magistrate no subjection is commanded, nor is any due; nor are the people forbidden to resist such authority; for in so doing, they do not resist the power nor the magistracy, as they are here excellently well described; but they resist a robber, a tyrant, an enemy, who, if he may notwithstanding, in some sense, be called a magistrate upon this account only, because he has power in his hands—by the same reason, the *devil* may be called a magistrate."

D.—Page 135.

As to the true origin of the Roman power, it is stated in Rev. xiii. 5,—"And the dragon gave him his power and state and great authority." On this *Dr. Junkin* says:

"Now the source of this power is pointed out. The dragon gave it to him: Diabolus formed this city and government for himself."

Dr. Scott says:

"The dragon may here mean either the devil, or the *devil's vicegerent*, the idolatrous Roman Empire.— So that when another idolatrous persecuting power had succeeded to that of the heathen emperors, then 'the dragon' had transferred his dominion to 'the beast,' or the devil had appointed another vicegerent, and all the world knows that this occurred to the history of the Roman Empire, Pagan and Papal."

Dr. Junkin adds:

"The Scripture account of absolute despotism (he might have said of all godless and Christless power,) is, that Satan gave it, and the *blasphemous slander of God* is the argument by which the doctrine of legitimacy is sustained from the Bible. 'Our power is of God.' 'The powers that be are ordained of God,'— therefore iron-handed despotism is a divine institution. This is the conclusion of its friends, but the word of truth proclaims it to be from below. The same kind of logic will prove the devil's own usurpations to be right and proper . . . The fallacy lies here in a false assumption. Paul says, 'The powers that be,' εχουσιαι, that is, *civil government*, is an ordinance of God; and the assumption is that it means arbitrary power—might without right. This is the logic by which Diabolus has blasphemed the Creator for a score of centuries." (See Lectures on Revelation, pp. 209, 210.)

E.—Page 150.

The arrogance of the Papists, both in England and in this country, is already beginning to awaken doubts whether after all it is safe to admit the votaries of superstition, and the subjects of such a spiritual despotism, to the full enjoyment of political rights among a Protestant people. God will yet avenge, and by the Papists themselves, as his instruments, nations that have not only given equal honour and protection to Christ's church and her anti-Christian counterfeit, but have boasted of this as a suitable display of liberality.

Dr. Junkin says:

"The grand defect in the bond of our national union is the absence of the recognition of God as the Governor of this world. We have omitted—may it not be said, refused?—to own Him whose head wears many crowns, as having any right of dominion over us. The constitution of the United States contains no express recognition of the being of a God; much less an acknowledgment that *The Word of God* sways the sceptre of universal dominion. This is our grand national sin of omission. This gives the infidel occasion to glory, and has no small influence in fostering infidelity in affairs of state, and among political men. That the nation will be blessed with peace and prosperity continuously, until this defect be remedied, no Christian philosopher expects. For this national insult, the Governor of the universe will lift again and again his rod of iron over our heads, until we be affrighted, and give this glory to his name.— (Lectures on Revelation, pp. 280–1.)